A SPECIAL FATE

A SPECIAL FATE

CHIUNE SUGIHARA: HERO OF THE HOLOCAUST

ALISON LESLIE GOLD

SCHOLASTIC INC.

New York Toronto London Auckland Sydney
Mexico City New Delhi Hong Kong

ISBN 0-439-25968-1

12 11 10 9 8 7 6 5 4 3 2 1   0 1 2 3 4 5/0

Printed in the U.S.A.   40

First Scholastic paperback printing, December 2000

Text set in Joanna MT 13/18 pt.
Book design by David Caplan
Cover photograph courtesy of Sugihara Family/Eric Saul, Curator

Dedication

This book is dedicated to Masha, Solly, and Yukiko. It is also dedicated to the memory of the Jewish people of Lithuania and Poland who were so cruelly obliterated during World War II.

A SPECIAL FATE

Chiune (Chee-YU-nay) Sugihara was 5′5″ tall. He combed his luxuriant black hair neatly, parting it on the side. His face was broad, his eyes were dark, kind, and penetrating. His clothes were tailored and suave; he was every inch the diplomat. In every surviving photograph, his full lips are set in a small smile.

Leon Ilutovicz, a lawyer from Warsaw, Poland, remembers the morning of August 2, 1940, in Kaunas, Lithuania, when his life was saved by Consul Sugihara. After Sugihara handwrote a visa for Japan into his passport, Sugihara smiled reassuringly at him.

Why would a career diplomat act in direct violation of official government policy? Why would such an official person sacrifice his entire career, his future, and the future of his family, to help desperate people who were being shunned by almost every other official and government throughout the world?

Is it possible, since *one* individual, like Hitler, is capable of so much *evil*, that *one* individual can also be capable of so much *good*? Can *good* in any way neutralize *evil*? These are the questions that I pondered when I discovered Chiune Sugihara's story.

I was fortunate to meet Chiune's widow, Yukiko, when she was eighty-four. In the years since Mr. Sugihara's death, she has dedicated her life to preserving his memory and the memory of his heroic deeds. Yukiko is a poetic and beautiful woman about five feet tall with light brown eyes. She welcomed my interest and answered my questions thoughtfully.

What better way, I decided, to enhance the story of Chiune and Yukiko for young readers than to weave in stories of actual young people who were caught in the rising flood of Hitler's hate and whose fate intersected with Sugihara? I found two people — Masha Bernstein and Solly Ganor — who were children in 1940. Both were Sugihara visa recipients and were willing to lend their often gruesome memories to this book.

In 1940, when Hitler's army attacked her city of Warsaw, Poland, Masha was a headstrong nine-year-old with braids who lived with her journalist father and dressmaker mother. Masha made a great subject to interview since her memory is extremely detailed and rich.

Solly Ganor also has a remarkable memory. He was born into a big, loving family in Kaunas, Lithuania. He has been extremely gracious in his willingness to help with this book. He was eleven years old when the war began in Europe in 1939. Solly summed up both his and Masha's experience very well when he commented, "In one moment I went from being a slightly spoiled, secure, normal boy to being a hunted animal."

Masha and Solly were two of the millions of people hunted like animals by Hitler and his helpers. Because of Chiune Sugihara's courage during this dark and brutal time, about 6,000 human beings, Masha included, were able to escape before the trap closed.

If you think that one good person can't morally offset one bad person, then think again. Think of Chiune Sugihara, the quiet Japanese diplomat, weeding his herb garden on a dewy morning in the summer of 1940 in Kaunas, Lithuania, as the world was igniting into flame. Think of his smile as, against official policy, he carefully handwrote and signed a visa that gave Leon Ilutovicz and thousands of others a reprieve from almost certain death.

1

The baby that was born on the very first day, January 1 of the new century, 1900, was a boy. He was born on an especially cold winter day in a small town named Yaotsu on one of the straggling chains of islands in the Far East known as Japan. The boy was named Chiune Sugihara.

There is a bit of Japanese folklore that made Chiune's parents think that perhaps their son might be special. It's believed that during particularly cold winter nights in Japan, a Snow Woman may appear dressed in white. She is an apparition, pale and cold like the snow, and is blamed for mysterious happenings.

Sometimes, people say, the Snow Woman appears

with a new winter baby, a baby like Chiune, in her arms. This baby is meant to have a very special fate. Perhaps their son Chiune Sugihara was meant to do something special during his life.

Summer in Yaotsu was boiling hot, so the large Sugihara family visited Grandpa and Grandma in the mountains to cool off in the pine and bamboo woods.

Chiune had five brothers and one sister. He and his brother Toyoaki liked to fish in the river. First they'd dig in the mud for fat worms to use as bait. Because they had no fishing lines, they'd wait for a horse and buggy to pass by, then they'd enrage the horse by pulling hairs from its tail, using long sticks of bamboo as snags.

The horse would bolt, but before the driver of the buggy could admonish the children, they would run away. These strong horsehairs were used as fishing lines to catch trout and other tasty fish that swam in the Kiso River. Even as a small boy, Chiune was a strong swimmer who could cross the entire width of the Kiso, which nestles beside Yaotsu.

Late in the day, after fishing, Chiune and the other children played a new game that had come to Japan from America. It was called "baseball" in English and "yakyuu" in Japanese, and young Sugihara was a natural player. Even though old-fashioned people referred to baseball as "the pickpocket's sport," he especially loved stealing home. They feared that "stealing" would corrupt their youth. Unlike American baseball uniforms, Japanese children wore brightly colored kimonos and clogs that made running difficult.

At the end of the day, tired and hungry from fishing and baseball, Chiune and his friends often took the short route back home across the rice paddies. They passed workers who were bent over cultivating the rice. These workers wore broad-brimmed straw hats and had rush mats tied on their backs to protect them from the strong sun.

Not so far away from Yaotsu, the Russo-Japanese War was being fought. Both Russia and Japan had imperialistic designs on Manchuria and Korea. Japan had attacked the city in Southern Manchuria called Port Arthur in May 1904, starting the war. Although the Japanese were happy because their army had captured Port Arthur and defeated the Russians at Mukden, many boys from Yaotsu had died. The whole town mourned the ash-filled urns, which were sent back to Yaotsu instead of their young sons.

Chiune's father, Mitsugoro Sugihara, was the Emperor's local tax collector. His mother, Yatsu, was the town beauty and had come from Samurai ancestry. Samurai had long been known as great warriors and aristocrats. Chiune admired the Samurai spirit, so he pleased his parents by throwing himself into his studies and bringing home report cards with very high grades.

Japanese children were taught a code in school. It had three laws: (a) *Do not be a burden to others;* (b) *Take care of others;* (c) *Do not expect rewards for your goodness.* Chiune memorized these laws and could say them by heart. But, he wondered, would he be able to live up to such high ideals?

Two earth-shattering events marked Chiune's early years. In 1910, his father began to work for the Japanese government in faraway Korea. From then on, his father was rarely at home. And, in 1912, on July 30, Emperor Mutsuhito of Japan died. Within two years the two men he idolized most had been taken away from him.

Some people in Japan believe that the spirit departs from the body at the time of death and takes the form of a bluish-white ball of fire with a tail. After the Emperor's death, many claimed to have seen his spirit hovering over rooftops at night, or thought they'd seen the Emperor's spirit in shooting stars. Chiune kept a watchful eye open in case he, too, got a glimpse of the Emperor's spirit.

Mitsugoro Sugihara left government service in 1915 because he'd developed an interest in speculating in Korea. He did not return to Japan. Instead he opened an inn in the Korean countryside outside of the city of Seoul.

In spite of the physical distance between them, Chiune's father was determined that his son would become a doctor. But, as Chiune got a little older and went to high school, he realized that he did not want to be a doctor at all. He wanted to become a teacher. When he admitted this to his father, his father became furious.

2

For the next several years, Chiune and his father fought over whether or not he would become a doctor. As he grew older and stronger, he became more determined to fulfill his own dream and not the dream of his father.

Things came to a head when Chiune refused to answer questions on the exam that would admit him to medical school. Leaving the entire examination blank, he was given a failing grade. Father and son had one final, very bitter argument. Outraged and hurt, Mitsugoro cut off his son's allowance.

Chiune traveled to Tokyo and enrolled in Waseda University in April 1919. He had to find a way to support himself. Although he found odd jobs delivering newspapers, working as a longshoreman, and tutoring other students, he couldn't make enough money and was dropped from the school in November.

He was nineteen years old. He was on his own and had no idea how he would survive. One day he saw an ad in the newspaper for students interested in studying abroad, with the goal of working for the Foreign Ministry. How to qualify? By passing an examination. How to live? A subsidy would be given. Successful completion of the study would offer a diplomatic career and travel aboard. Although this meant giving up his dream of becoming a teacher, it offered him independence from his father and promised an interesting life in exotic places.

After intensive study, he took the examination. He passed and now had to choose a language of specialization. He had taken an interest in Russian literature and liked Russian vodka, too, so he chose Russian. In October 1919, he was given a scholarship of 1,600 yen by the Foreign Ministry to go to faraway Harbin, China, to study at the Harbin School.

Harbin is on the Sungari River in Manchuria, in northeast China. Because the railroad had been built through Harbin at the end of the 1800s, it had become a cosmopolitan and international transportation center, sometimes called the "Paris of the Orient." Its population was about 500,000 at the time — 339,000 Chinese; 120,000 Russians; 13,000 Japanese; and various Europeans.

Mixed in with the Christians and Buddhists in Harbin was a group of exotic people that Chiune had never encountered in Japan. These were Jewish people. About 13,000 Jews lived in Harbin and seemed to have a hard lot, since they were often treated badly for no apparent reason.

Chiune lived in the Japanese district near Uchastkovaya Street. Because he was such a perfectionist in his studies, he began to attach a pen and a small bottle of ink to a rope and tie the rope around his ear. Thus, at any moment, he could reach for the pen, dip it into the ink, and make a note.

People laughed at this eccentricity. But when they saw that this young man was able to memorize an entire page from the Russian dictionary, people stopped laughing at his dangling pen and ink. They took him more seriously.

Very quickly, Sugihara became fluent in Russian. He was also learning other languages — English, Chinese, French, and German.

Except for a year of military training and service, Sugihara remained in Harbin and finished his studies. He was so good at Russian that he was asked to stay on and teach it. He was also asked to play first base with the Auroras, a baseball team made up of railroad and consulate employees.

At night, Sugihara would stroll with friends through Harbin, along Kitayskaya Street in the Russian quarter, which was inhabited by Chinese and Russians, past the Russian Orthodox Church and a Jewish synagogue. He'd sit in a noisy cafe with friends, have a glass of vodka, and practice his Russian. Sometimes he saw Jewish refugees from Russia walking toward the railroad station. These people were trying to get to America by crossing into China.

Sugihara's mother died in 1921 in Korea, where she had gone to join her husband, but because Chiune was far away, he could not attend her funeral. Although it was rare for a Japanese man to show private feelings, Chiune wept publicly. It didn't seem particularly strange to people he knew, as he was an unusual individual who wore a pen dangling from his ear.

In 1921 Sugihara became a clerk and interpreter at the Japanese Ministry of Foreign Affairs. He also taught Russian part-time, which pleased him very much. The school's motto was: *Do much for others and expect little in return.*

After intensive study of the Russian language, which led to a deepening admiration for the Russian culture, he decided to convert to the Russian Orthodox religion. While Sugihara undertook this religious commitment respectfully, he kept intact many of the principles of his upbringing — such as the Japanese ideas of responsibility and virtue; Shinto beliefs in oneness of the spirit and obedience; and Buddhist teachings of compassion and self-denial.

3

Chiune Sugihara was sent to Tokyo by the Ministry of Foreign Affairs. He was shocked to see that nearly half of Tokyo had been destroyed by a devastating earthquake in 1923 and that almost 100,000 people had died. Next, he was posted to Manchuria, which the Japanese had conquered and renamed Manchukuo. He quickly rose in the ministry, becoming Vice Chief of the Foreign Ministry of Manchukuo.

In 1935 he met an idealistic twenty-one-year-old girl named Yukiko Kikuchi. She had light brown eyes and wavy hair and was well-educated. He was charmed that she wrote a short form of poetry called tanka and had even had a few poems published. After getting to know her and falling in love, Chiune asked Yukiko to marry him.

Yukiko asked him if he thought she'd make a good wife for him. He explained that she seemed like a person who could adjust well to living in a foreign country and would be an ideal wife for a diplomat.

She accepted with pleasure.

Chiune was thirteen years older than Yukiko. He was handsome, had a lovely smile, and always listened attentively to her, which was not always the way Japanese men treated women. His nature was kind, considerate of others, and always gentle. They married and, to please him, Yukiko converted to the Russian Orthodox religion.

Their little son, Hiroki, was soon born. A short posting at the Japanese embassy in Russia followed.

In 1937, a new assignment came through. The Sugiharas were to be posted in Helsinki, Finland. They decided to bring Yukiko's younger sister, Setsuko, with them so that she could keep Yukiko company, help with the baby, and also study abroad.

Because of some diplomatic tensions at the time between Japan and the Soviet Union, the Sugiharas had to travel the long way around to Helsinki instead of traveling west through Russia into Finland.

They went eastward from Japan to Seattle, crossed

the United States to New York, and sailed across the Atlantic on the grand luxury liner *Bremen*, which flew the red-and-black, crooked-cross flag of the new German government being led by a man named Adolf Hitler. The other passengers were astonished to see Yukiko dressed in a kimono at meals, as many of them had never seen a Japanese person.

The ship docked in Germany. Finally a train and a smaller ship took them to Finland.

Wanting to be the perfect wife of a diplomat, Yukiko studied German and French in Helsinki. She took etiquette and dance lessons. Although she usually dressed like a Western woman, she still sometimes wore Japanese kimonos. One time she wore a purple kimono to a gala. Her bright robes and beautiful face brought her much attention at receptions until she became pregnant with a second child, and, being old-fashioned, stopped attending public events.

After Chiaki, another boy, was born, the growing family acquired a summer cottage in a white birch forest outside of Helsinki. It was here that Chiune learned how to drive, although as a diplomat, he was provided with a chauffeur. One night in a panic, the chauffeur told Yukiko that the family car had been stolen!

She went to find her husband to report the theft,

but when she glanced out the window, she was astonished to see the car coming up the driveway. Yukiko watched as Chiune got out of the car. He was smiling contentedly. Later he confided that he very much wanted to drive and he'd been driving secretly at night.

Yukiko laughed when he told her this because she had already noticed that his personality was such that he always did what he wanted to do.

Despite growing tensions in Europe because of Hitler's annexation of Austria, and the premonition that war was coming to Europe, the Sugiharas enjoyed the summer of 1939 with their playful little sons at their country cottage.

The nights of midnight sun meant that the sky stayed light all night in Finland in summer. Sometimes Chiune and Yukiko couldn't sleep and would take walks to a nearby lake in the middle of the night. The midnight sun was eerie but beautiful. At moments, it seemed as if time was standing still.

Abruptly, the spell was broken when Consul Sugihara received an official order from his government. He was to be posted in Lithuania. Neither Yukiko nor Chiune knew much about that small country, except that it was on the Baltic Sea north of

Poland, south of Latvia, and across from Sweden. It was known as the "land of amber" because rare and mysterious amber could be found on its seashore. The city to which they were to go in Lithuania was named Kaunas.

CHAPTER

On *September* 1, 1939, Adolf Hitler's army attacked Poland with tanks, bombers, armored trucks, and soldiers on horseback. World War II had begun.

In the city of Warsaw, Poland, Masha Bernstein, an eigh-year-old with blond braids and blue eyes, lived with her parents, Matvey and Zelda. Her father was a journalist and writer. They were Jewish and lived in an ordinary six-story apartment building.

When the attack started, men between the ages of sixteen and sixty were advised by the Polish government to leave the city so that they would not be captured by the German army. Thinking that Hitler's army would never get to Warsaw, and that his absence would be temporary, Matvey left the city.

But no matter what, the family agreed, if they were separated from one another, they'd find their way to the small town in the northeast of Poland named Byten and wait for one another. This was the town where both Matvey and Zelda had lived before coming to Warsaw.

After Matvey had gone, Masha and Zelda lived in fear. When bombs began to drop on Warsaw, everyone ran down into their cellars in terror. Although neither Zelda nor Masha was injured in the bombing, their entire street was leveled and only one section of their building remained standing.

Masha and Zelda dug their way out of the cellar and climbed over rubble and barricades which were being constructed against tanks. These barricades were made from furniture, overturned carts, and dead horses. They saw that the city of Warsaw was on fire. Mrs. Bernstein grabbed Masha by the hand and they ran down Swieto-Jierska Street between walls of flame.

It was night. Everywhere, people were running. No one knew where to go, but ran nonetheless. As a crowd ran toward them, another mass of disoriented, panicked people ran in different directions. Walls of flames were shooting up on both sides of the street.

In the confusion, Masha noticed a bearded man who was pulling a girl of six or seven by the hand. The man held brass candlesticks in his hand and had a goose-down pillow under his arm. There was so much confusion that even though the little girl was clutching his hand, the man shouted her name, which was Rochele.

Soon the Germans had defeated the pathetically under-equipped Polish army. They marched into, and occupied Warsaw. Food quickly became hard to find. Zelda went out into the street and sold things in order to buy food. One time she could only find rancid herring and rotten pumpkin. As hungry as she was, Masha refused to eat.

Winter was coming. Because most of their things had been destroyed in the bombing, Masha needed a winter coat. Unfortunately, items like coats were almost impossible to find. Mrs. Bernstein, who had been a professional dressmaker, found a rug and made a winter coat out of it for Masha. She found a belt belonging to her husband for the coat. Zelda also found four buttons, but before she could sew them onto the coat, she decided that they'd better get out of Warsaw and into the countryside. Because of Hitler's anti-Jewish policies, the Germans had immediately begun to round up Jews.

Zelda Bernstein thought carefully about what to

take into the country. She didn't have jewelry or much money, so she took needles, thread, salt, matches, and bed sheets, which she hoped she'd be able to trade with peasants for food and shelter. She took along the four buttons to sew onto Masha's coat. The only thing Masha took was her doll.

While the bombing continued, Zelda and Masha left their bombed-out apartment and ran to the home of a family they knew who owned a restaurant. These people let them stay with them. Zelda bought bowls of soup from their restaurant. When the little girl of the house reached for Masha's doll, Zelda wrenched the doll from Masha's hand and gave it to the little girl to placate her. She didn't want to cause any friction whatsoever until they could arrange to get out of the city entirely.

Because of the bombing, there was no water and no electricity. Because Masha was blond and looked like most Christian Polish children, she could go and wait in line to get their ration of bread and margarine.

Winter, always nasty in Poland, arrived. Mrs. Bernstein found a Polish peasant who, for a price, would take them out into the country. She hoped they could get to Byten. Masha and Zelda sat all day in icy sleet and rain in the peasant's wagon while he collected enough people to fill it. Masha had the mumps and a high fever and some kind of sickness from malnutrition, which caused her mouth to be covered with sores. She felt terrible.

Finally, there were six children, three women, and an old Jewish man in the wagon. The peasant brought his whip down hard on the horse's back.

5

The peasant took them out of the city and, to their horror, right to Gestapo headquarters. He slyly told the Gestapo officer that he had a bunch of Jews hiding in his wagon.

The Gestapo lined them up, children included. They were terrified. Each person was given a number — 1, 2, 3, 4, 5, 6, 7, 8, 9, 10. At dawn, the Germans shot numbers 1, 3, 5, 7, and 9. Masha had number 6, her mother had number 4.

Then, without any explanation, the Gestapo let them go.

Masha and Zelda walked away by themselves in the direction of the Russian border. Her mother told

Masha that in case they were caught, the story Masha should remember was that Zelda was taking her home to their family in the provinces. Zelda told her that the Russians had warm hearts and if they were caught by them, Masha should cry.

For the next few weeks they walked mostly at night. They went through swamps and fields and woods. In the day they hid in haystacks and ravines, always avoiding villages with barking dogs. Even though she was still sick, Masha carried a knapsack and a satchel. Zelda carried a suitcase and another knapsack. In the evening Zelda would knock on doors of various small huts where peasants lived. She'd ask for a night's shelter. She'd also ask if they wanted to have a cow milked or wanted her to dig up potatoes.

Often the peasants would slam the door in her face, but sometimes they wouldn't. For money, they sometimes let Masha come into the house because she was blond and blended with the Polish children. They made Zelda sleep in the barn because they thought she was a Jew.

When they got to the border between the German part of Poland and the Russian part, the German soldiers raised the barrier. Between the two parts of occupied Poland was a vast and barren no-man's-land. It was several hundred yards wide and ran for miles and miles, with a line of trees that led into a forest along one side. Masha and Zelda joined hundreds of other refugees in the open field. Everyone thought that soon they would be safe.

From out of the forest came Russian soldiers on horseback with red stars on their peaked gray military hats. They wore bandoliers, which were crisscrossed belts of bullets, and carried bayonets. The soldiers shouted at the refugees to return to the German side, so the crowd rushed back to the German barrier, but it was closed. The Germans wouldn't let anyone back through.

People began wandering along the strip of no-man's-land. Some people gave up hope and sat dejected. As food and water ran out, many died from hunger and cold.

Masha and her mother walked away from the other refugees. Soon they were by themselves. A Polish peasant woman leading a horse-drawn wagon of hay told them to climb in and hide in the hay.

The woman hid them in the cellar of her house for three days, even though the penalty in German-occupied Poland for helping Jews meant death. The kind woman fed them, cared for the sick little girl, and let them rest. When Zelda tried to pay her, she refused the money, saying that she was only doing her Catholic duty.

After they had rested, they again walked across no-man's-land. Suddenly, out of the treeline came a single Russian soldier, a boy about seventeen years old, with his bayonet ready. He shouted for them to go back to the German side or he'd shoot.

Mrs. Bernstein set her black valise down on the ground. Tired and almost without hope, Zelda told him in Russian that he might as well shoot her. She'd rather a Russian shoot her than a German.

Masha remembered that her mother had told her that if they met the Russians, she should start crying, so she started crying. Her mother turned to her and in a comforting voice, begged her to stop crying, calling her Mashinka.

Mashinka was the diminutive of her name, which is the Russian version of Mary, a popular name in Russia. The soldier wanted to know since when did Polish people give their children Russian names.

The soldier was bewildered. He told them that he had a sister called Masha. Same name, same age, same braids parted in the middle like Masha. If he shot Masha it would be like shooting his sister.

The soldier took them across the border into the Russian part of Poland, which was now joined to the larger Soviet Union, to military headquarters. They were given bread, tea, butter, and apples, while he and the other Russian soldiers serenaded them with songs. In the morning they put Masha and Zelda on a military truck, which took them to the train station at Bialystok, a town northeast of Warsaw.

After days of waiting, Masha and Zelda squeezed through the crowd onto the train. They found a seat in the last car. Exhausted, they waited for the train to start. As they waited, Mrs. Bernstein suddenly became alert. She told Masha that she thought she had heard someone calling their names.

They looked hopefully out the train window. For a moment Zelda thought she saw her husband Matvey on the platform. But the figure disappeared into the mob, the engine started, and the train left the chaotic station.

At last, they arrived at their destination, Byten. In that small town, and in nearby towns, lived both sets of Masha's grandparents, uncles and aunts, and forty-five cousins. True to his word, a few days afterward, her father arrived. And when he told them about his own travails — going back and forth to dangerous

Warsaw through Bialystok — they realized that, yes, it had indeed been him at the train station calling their names.

Before they could enjoy the reunion, a childhood friend of Matvey told him that it was unsafe to stay in the town. So, before they'd even rested, they were wrapped up in bandages, hidden in an ambulance, and driven out of town.

Masha asked her father where they were going. He told her that they were going to Vilna. When Masha looked mystified, he told her that Vilna was in the small, independent country of Lithuania, which was three or four days travel from Byten. He told her that it was a Jewish center of learning and that for the time being Jews were safe in Vilna.

CHAPTER

6

Sugihara *and his family arrived* in Kaunas, also known as Kovno, Lithuania, in late summer 1939. Kaunas was a provincial city. They lived in the modern, newly constructed Hotel Metropolis. At first the weather was mild, the days were long. In the center of the city were wide streets and tall, bushy chestnut trees.

The chief landmark of the city was the white Peter and Paul Church with the highest spire in Kaunas. The spire could be seen from far away. St. George's Church, the Russian Orthodox church with a large cupola that glowed when the sun hit it, was on Dubijos Street near the railway station.

Because Lithuania is so far north, the sun didn't set

until around eleven at night and then a silvery twilight tinted the sky all night. The land around was flat except for steep hills along the wide Niemunas River. The city was ringed by ancient castles and fortresses.

Chiune's title was vice consul to Lithuania. He cabled his government: *I searched hard for a house and finally found one. It is at the eastern part of the city near the houses of ambassadors.*

When his choice of a residence was given approval, the Sugiharas moved into their new house at 30 Vaizgantas Street. It had a stucco façade; a wrought iron, lattice gate; and a curved staircase leading to its entrance. They moved in on October 17, and then the Japanese Consulate was officially opened. Because number 30 was at the top of a hill, the quaint city of Kaunas, with its church spires, Gothic roofs, many chestnut trees, and the river, could be seen from the windows.

Chiune hired a valet, a secretary, a butler, and other staff. He hired a chauffeur named Borislav who kept his black Buick shined. The consulate also had a little garden. Sugihara himself planned to tend the garden because Mrs. Sugihara, who enjoyed shopping and organizing the household, didn't enjoy gardening.

Often Mr. Sugihara took his family out in the car for

motor trips. On these rides they drove down Laisves Aleya, the wide, main boulevard, past shops and restaurants. They passed two Jewish synagogues that dated from 1600 on Lia des Gatue Street.

Just outside of town was an astonishing sight known as the Hill of Crosses. The Hill of Crosses was a hill covered by thousands of crosses — large and tiny, devotional and memorial. Some were finely carved. The hill had originally been a fortification. The tradition of erecting the crosses there began in the 14th century and had continued to the present.

Old women wearing black sold crosses and rosaries at the gate to the hill. The place was essentially silent except for the rattling of crosses in the wind.

As the Sugiharas drove out into the Lithuanian countryside, they passed the forts built by a Russian czar in the early part of the century. They passed old wooden farmsteads, summer cottages, and woods. In the countryside, after the start of the war, these roads were clogged with refugees fleeing the advancing German army that had quickly conquered and occupied nearby Poland. Feeling anxious but helpless to assist them, Sugihara passed families and single refugees walking toward Kaunas.

Tired refugees who'd walked these roads — mostly

Polish Jews — were also filling Kaunas's streets. Kaunas's very large Jewish population was doing their best to shelter and to feed them. In fact, of the 120,000 people living in Kaunas, 30,000 were Jewish. The newly arriving Jews were swelling this number every day.

CHAPTER

7

Solly Ganor was eleven years old when the war began. Some of Solly's family had lived in Kaunas for generations. Solly and his big family followed every detail of the widening war. They had special anxiety because they were Jewish. One day in December 1939, Solly's mother sent him across the Niemunas River to buy a bucket of apples. She was starting to bake goodies for Chanukah, the Jewish "Festival of Lights."

To cross the river Solly had to take a barge. The barge was made of empty barrels lashed together on which stood a wooden platform surrounded by a railing. An old Lithuanian named Kazys ran the barge by means of a metal cable strung across the river, which he hauled hand over hand.

31

That day a soldier on a motorcycle arrived at the ferry. He shouted out that he had an important message to deliver. Kazys screamed back at him demanding that he take his stinking machine off his boat. The soldier drew his pistol and demanded that Kazys shut up and get out of his way. Didn't Kazys know there was a war on or was he a stupid old man?

Solly drew back fearfully at the sight of the pistol, not only because some of the apples were stolen from an orchard but because he was Jewish, a people not much liked by many Lithuanians.

Solly's mother, Rebecca, and his Aunt Anushka were part of a committee that had formed to help the refugees in Kaunas. And, in fact, at almost every meal at the Ganors', refugees shared the table. When Solly brought home the apples, he was introduced to two new refugees who were staying with them — Mr. Rosenblat and his plump daughter, Lea.

His mother whispered to him that she'd given his room to the Rosenblats. When Solly showed irritation, Rebecca shook her finger at him, reminding him that he would have to make sacrifices, too. After all, those people had lost everything — their jobs, their homes.

Of course Solly felt guilty. He promised his mother that he'd make it up to them.

He immediately made good on his promise when two ladies who were making a collection for the refugees rang their doorbell. Solly reached deep into his pants pocket, and pulled out 10 lit, which he had been given as Chanukah *gelt* by a relative. He gallantly offered it as a donation to the cause.

As soon as lunch was finished, he left the house and walked toward the city center. He regretted his grandiose sacrifice. A new Laurel and Hardy movie, which he'd planned to see, was showing at the Metropolitan Theater. What to do now, with no money in his pocket?

Aunt Anushka came to mind. She was always a soft touch. Solly walked in the direction of Aunt Anushka's fancy shop, which was in the best part of Kaunas. Imported specialties were sold at the shop — caviar, champagne, good cheese, Swiss chocolate. Foreign dignitaries, ambassadors, and rich ladies shopped there.

As Solly walked, wet snowflakes began to spin and fall onto his dark hair and to the ground. He passed Jewish homes like his own, and he could see Chanukah menorahs through the windows. At the Christian section, he saw Christmas trees instead.

When he entered Aunt Anushka's shop, he noticed a well-dressed gentleman speaking with Aunt Anushka.

When Aunt Anushka saw Solly, she guessed that he wanted to go to the movies, and he needed a lit or two. Aunt Anushka laughed. She knew him so well. Then she introduced Solly to His Excellency, the consul from Japan, Mr. Sugihara.

Mr. Sugihara looked at Solly in a friendly way. Sugihara reached into his pocket and took out a coin. He said to Solly that since this was Chanukah, please consider him an uncle and please call him *Sempo*, which was an easier, warmer name, a variation of Chiune. He held out the coin.

Solly was so eager, he reached out to grab the shiny coin, then hesitated. Sugihara smiled, and pushed it into his hand. Solly blurted out an invitation to Mr. Sugihara to come to his family's Chanukah party on Saturday. Then he underscored the invitation by reminding Sugihara that since he was Uncle *Sempo* he would be expected.

They laughed together. Sugihara confessed that he'd never been to a Chanukah party and bowed, accepting the invitation.

CHAPTER

8

On Saturday, a dry, frosty day, the Chanukah celebration started first thing in the morning with freshly baked rolls drowned in strawberry preserves, mushroom omelets, and hot chocolate. Mrs. Ganor cooked all day and added the big extensions to the mahogany table before she covered it with a special white tablecloth.

Mr. Rosenblat and his daughter, Lea; Aunt Dobbe and Uncle Jochil; Cousin Miriam; Aunt Leena; Uncle Jacob; Solly's sister Fanny; his older brother Herman; Solly; and Solly's father Chaim were sitting in the living room when Aunt Anushka and Mr. and Mrs. Sugihara arrived. Sugihara wore a dressy striped suit, and his wife Yukiko wore a chic black dress.

The Sugiharas brought a whiff of elegance in with them.

Rebecca Ganor ushered everyone to the long table, and little Lea was invited to light the candles and say the opening words: *Praised are You, Lord our God, ruler of the Universe, who performed miracles for our ancestors. It is You who lights my lamp; Lord, my God, light up my darkness.*

Mr. and Mrs. Sugihara listened attentively to the story of Judah Maccabee. Then, wonderful food filled the table — veal with roasted potatoes and Japanese-style duck in orange sauce, which had been brought by Anushka from her shop. Everyone ate too much.

Afterward, Mr. Rosenblat began telling about his harrowing escape from Poland. He described the bombings in Warsaw and his wife's death. He told of how Jews were being terrorized by the Nazis, arrested, and sent to concentration camps. He became so upset that he started to cry. Everyone looked at him with compassion but also dismay.

Rosenblat begged Sugihara to get him a visa to get out of Kaunas. He confessed that he'd been asking at every consulate during his travels, but no one was willing to help him.

Sugihara looked grim. He explained that it was doubtful that his government would allow him to issue such a visa but to please come to see him. He turned to Mr. Ganor and asked if he had plans or the desire to leave Lithuania.

Mr. Ganor replied that he had a business in Lithuania which he hesitated to leave. Sugihara spoke carefully, looking at Mr. Ganor directly, intensely in the eye. He suggested that Mr. Ganor not worry too much about his business.

The party had turned gloomy. To lighten things up, Uncle Jacob pulled his harmonica from his pocket and blew a few notes, suggesting some Chanukah songs. Lea began to sing. Shakily, Solly and the others joined in.

As the Sugiharas were putting on their coats, Mr. Sugihara turned to Solly and told him that he'd noticed that Solly collected stamps. He then invited Solly to visit him at the consulate and he would give Solly some Japanese stamps for his collection.

Chaim and Rebecca Ganor opened the front door for their honored guests. Snow was falling heavily. Solly was excited by the idea of Japanese stamps.

The Jewish hosts watched as their elegant yet convivial Japanese guests pulled their overcoats around them and stepped out into the thick, swirling snow.

9

Although the stunning streamers of the northern lights made an appearance in the night sky, the Lithuanian winter was long and dark. Morning came late and it grew dark again by early afternoon. The naked trees were stark against the murky daylight.

As frigid temperatures in Lithuania went lower and lower, people wore long sheepskin coats and fur-trimmed boots in winter. Those who could afford it wore fur. Poor people wore shawls and blankets and wrapped themselves in newspapers and rags against the bitter cold.

On January 1, 1940, Chiune Sugihara turned forty. On January 15, the Soviet Union sent troops to tiny Lithuania, but promised it would remain an independent republic. Because Chiune was fluent in Russian, he had no trouble dealing with the new Russian administration.

Combining work with pleasure, Chiune and Yukiko would often bundle up the children and drive out into the countryside. Chiune took photographs. He gathered information about troop movements and movements of military vehicles. He monitored various details of military importance for the Japanese government. Sometimes he dropped the family back home and drove off by himself to do more secret surveying for his government.

The Sugihara family lived on the first two floors of 30 Vaizgantas Street. Consul Sugihara's office was in the half-basement. There were now two maids and two consulate workers. One of these workers was a German named Wolfgang Gudze. The third floor of the building was rented out to Jadvyga Ulvydaite, an unhappy nineteen-year-old girl, who lived with her brother.

Occasionally during dark winter days, Sugihara's little sons would go upstairs and play with Jadvyga. There they'd eat delicious Lithuanian pancakes with cheese filling and jam. To thank Jadvyga, Sugihara had their maid bring ice cream upstairs to her as a gift.

One day Mr. Sugihara saw Jadvyga and stopped her.

He commented that she seemed very sad. Sooner or later, he promised, everything in her life would improve. Evil would be outweighed by good. He urged her not to surrender to despair.

In 1940, although the war hadn't come to Lithuania, Hitler had expanded the war front to the seas. Poland was subjugated, and German bombers were dropping bombs on England. The war was widening.

The ice on Lithuania's rivers began breaking up with loud cracking noises, and the snow began to melt. Quickly the streets of Kaunas became a mess of slush and mud. More and more refugees, mostly from Poland, poured into the city. Escape from Poland had become harder, and the refugees had all seen and experienced harsh conditions and shocking brutalities inflicted by the German Nazis against Jews, and against just about anyone who didn't agree with the Nazis.

At the earliest hint of spring, musty bedding that was being aired out hung from every window and balcony. First thing in the morning, before he began his work, Chiune Sugihara began to prepare his little garden for planting. People who passed by could see him wearing knickerbockers and bending down. Some people would sometimes stare because they'd never seen a Japanese person before.

One afternoon after school, Solly Ganor — as invited — visited Mr. Sugihara at the consulate. Sugihara welcomed him warmly and invited him into his office. He pulled out an envelope from his desk drawer. Inside was a batch of Japanese stamps. Solly studied the exotic face on the stamps.

Mr. Sugihara informed Solly that he was looking at the Japanese Emperor's face. Then, Sugihara asked if Mr. Rosenblat and his little daughter had obtained an exit visa yet. Solly told him that they hadn't.

Sugihara's face was grave. They both knew that the situation was becoming more and more ominous, the refugees more menaced, the war in Europe getting worse. Solly didn't say so, but his parents were having discussions about whether or not to try to leave Lithuania, whether or not Mr. Ganor should try to sell his business at a loss. Mr. Ganor couldn't imagine that Hitler would dare to invade neutral Lithuania.

Sugihara asked Solly if he would take a message to his father. Solly nodded. Mr. Sugihara spoke directly and quietly; he asked that Solly give his father the message that the time to leave was now.

Solly turned white. Mr. Sugihara patted his head and underscored the message by repeating that he hoped Mr. Ganor would take his advice, for Solly's sake if not for his own.

CHAPTER

10

In *Kaunas, Yukiko gave birth* to a third son. He was named Haruki, which means Bright Spirit. He had long, dark eyelashes and was sweet and frail.

When Sugihara had first been assigned to open a Japanese consulate in Lithuania, he had considered sending his family back to Japan because of the tensions in Europe, but Yukiko had requested that she and the children accompany him to Kaunas, so that the family could stay together. Now, with the joy of the new baby, even with the growing tensions around them, the family was glad to be together in the house at 30 Vaizgantas Street on the hill.

Crocuses and daffodils sprouted in Sugihara's garden. After Denmark and Norway were attacked and occupied by Hitler, the president of Lithuania, Antanas Smetona, tried to encourage the population with speeches on the radio. Smetona assured the people that, despite the Russian troops and administration, Lithuania would remain independent; it would not be swallowed up either by Russia or by Germany.

When Easter came, Jadvyga showed the Sugihara children how Lithuanian children painted eggs with dyes. She used onion skins to shade eggs brown. That day children all over Kaunas as well as Sugihara's children rolled eggs and tried to hit other eggs. Afterward, Easter cake with raisins was served to them. Then the eggs were eaten and the crushed, painted shells were dropped on the ground.

In May 1940, the consulate was alerted when Hitler attacked Holland and then Belgium. In June, Hitler attacked France. At the same time severe storms — winds, downpours, thunder and lightning — pelted the fleeing refugees and also Sugihara's garden, punishing his delicate spring flowers. When the unstable weather ended, the clear, blue sky and warm sun signaled that summer was on its way.

Midsummer Night's Eve is the longest day of the year. It coincides with St. John's Day on June 24, which is a Lithuanian national holiday. On this holiday local people wearing oak and flower wreaths gather around bonfires and sing, dance, and drink beer. The Japanese consulate was shut for the holiday. Shops were shut, too.

All night and day, people strolled along the river or into the countryside, where bonfires blazed. Night never comes on this holiday. Instead, the fragrant, endless twilight lasts all night.

Local people call the holiday Rasos. It is a night with magical powers. Celebrants seek the mythical fern flower which, it is believed, only blooms that night. Anyone who finds this flower will have good luck. But it's also said that anyone who falls asleep on that special night might have an evil eye cast on him.

The Midsummer Night bonfires very much reminded Sugihara of a Japanese legend. The legend has it that any strange, rosy, pink fire sighted on a hill, or in a field, or beside a graveyard, has been lit by foxes. These fires are known as "foxfires" and augur strange events to come.

As Sugihara gazed out at the glowing bonfires from his hilltop, he sipped a glass of likeriai, a fruit liqueur drunk on this holiday. He felt a sudden chill. He shivered and wondered what unusual events were on their way.

Throughout the long, twilit night, ragged refugees speaking Yiddish, Russian, German, and Polish choked the narrow, curving roads that led into Kaunas, passing the festivities and bonfires. They came by train, by horse-drawn wagon, by auto, by foot.

CHAPTER

11

After Masha Bernstein *and her parents* got to Vilna (about 60 miles east of Kaunas), her father began to work for the Yiddish Research Institute known as YIVO. Vilna was a sprawling city with about four times the number of people of Kaunas, covering about 100 square miles. Someone gave Zelda a little portable Singer sewing machine so she could help support her family by sewing pajamas and shirts, and by making dresses.

Cosmopolitan, bustling Vilna was also called Wilno. About 90,000 Jews lived there and it was one of the great centers of Jewish study. Two rivers passed through the city — the Wilya and the Wilenka. Jewish refugees noticed that in the Jewish cemetery in Vilna there was a large white sculpture of an eagle. Its wings were spread but the right wing was cut off.

Masha went to school in Vilna and told everyone what she'd seen in Warsaw — German soldiers stopping old Jews and tearing chunks of beard from their faces; Poles pointing out Jews to the Germans and sometimes beating them up; women being forced to clean the cobbled streets with toothbrushes. Once, she'd seen a German soldier chop a finger off a woman in order to get her ring.

The teacher looked sternly at Masha and accused her of making up stories, of frightening both herself and the other children. The teacher could not believe that the Germans or some of the Poles could be so cruel.

Mrs. Bernstein made Masha a gray alpaca dress out of Grandma's Sabbath dress, which she had brought from Byten. Now Masha wore it with a little white collar every day because it was the only dress she had. The Bernsteins lived in a little cottage on the outskirts of Vilna. It had a garden in the back, where the family grew sunflowers, vegetables, and fruits. Thanks to the garden, there was a little extra food to eat.

Masha met another little girl who was also a refugee. Her name was Olenka. They met in the local communal soup kitchen. Olenka and Masha explored the garden on their knees, looking very closely at the earth, plants, stems, and at anthills because they were writing a book together called The Life of Ants.

Now that there was a little money coming in, Masha could go to the movies. She went to see Shirley Temple in The Little Princess, which was about a little girl named Sara whose father is sent off to fight in the Crimean War of the 1850s. The little girl is placed in a rich boarding school until a notice comes that her father has been killed. As a result, the little girl becomes a cleaning girl. One day she goes through a hospital ward of war wounded and hears someone calling her name. "Sara! Sara!" It's her father. He's alive after all. She dives into his arms.

Everyone in the theater cried. Sara's reunion reminded Masha of her own reunion with Matvey. Every day she was grateful that he'd returned to the family and that they were all together.

One day the three of them went to the movies to see Marie Antoinette, starring Tyrone Power and Norma Shearer. When they came out of the theater, they were shocked to see Russian tanks rolling down the street. Russia had taken over Lithuania. Fearful of what might come, everyone ran home to hoard whatever food they could.

Two months later, Matvey Bernstein was arrested as a political prisoner by the Russian secret police and was taken away.

Fearful that they would also be arrested, Mrs. Bernstein and Masha walked out of their apartment, leaving many of their possessions behind. They went to live on University Street, on the other side of the city, with a cousin who sold pianos and harpsichords. Fortunately, the cousin was willing to take them in.

They lived in a tiny room behind a large room used to store pianos. This room had dozens of upright and grand pianos. Their little sleeping room was the size of a broom closet, just large enough to hold a cot which they shared, sleeping head to foot. After they went to bed at night, the cousin moved a piano in front of their door, and when they woke up, he moved the piano aside to let them out.

For safety, Masha went to a different school. She registered using a new name. When she saw her former teacher, they both turned chalk-white. They were both afraid of betrayal. The teacher was afraid Masha would call her by her real name, and so was Masha, since both were using false names.

To appear patriotic, Masha joined the Young Pioneers, which was like the Girl Scouts. She learned to sing a song about the Russian Dictator, Joseph Stalin:

He is taller than the mountains,
He is deeper than the ocean . . .

Every morning Masha and Zelda would go and stand outside Lukishki Prison, waiting to get a message or food or winter clothing to imprisoned Matvey. At night, as Masha was going to sleep, her mother would tell her not to worry if she wasn't there when Masha woke up. She explained that she was taking the earliest train to Kaunas, the provincial capital, to visit consulates to try to get them a visa to go to America. She warned Masha not to speak of this to anyone, to trust no one. She said it again with emphasis, *zog gornisht*, trust no one!

CHAPTER

12

After the Soviet Union sent troops to Lithuania, Kaunas was no longer a diplomatic center. Some of the consulates there began closing.

Jewish refugees trapped in Kaunas with a few extra lit ate at the smoky, noisy Alexander Restaurant, which served cheap kosher food. Their passionate topic of conversation was escape routes. All escape routes were illegal, hazardous, or both. However, without a visa — either a transit visa "to pass through" or a regular visa — escape was impossible.

A visa is an official endorsement made on a passport, permitting the bearer to enter or pass through either the country named on the visa or the country issuing the visa. Anxiously, refugees debated whether it was possible to go overland through Russia to Odessa, then to Istanbul, and then on to Palestine by ship. And what about getting visas? It always came back to the need for a visa.

Even on the Sabbath, the discussion of visas continued. On the Sabbath, the Alexander served a special meal to its Jewish patrons. After baking slowly in the oven for almost an entire day and filling the Alexander with delicious smells, the traditional meal of meat with potatoes, beans, onions, and barley known as *cholent* was served. On other days, discussions were held while wolfing down inexpensive *gefilte fish, balan-dele* — stuffed cabbage roll — and *silke* — herring; or over bad coffee that tasted like chicory.

Some people argued, Why not stay in Lithuania? At least Lithuania was relatively safe, bearably comfortable. And besides, even if they *could* get out, no countries wanted them. There was nowhere they could go without a visa except maybe to Asia, where they could then attempt to escape to Palestine or America or Canada or other faraway parts of the world.

But the Alexander customers were the lucky ones. Cheap as it was, most refugees were too poor to buy a meal at a restaurant and were living off the charity of

Chiune and Yukiko Sugihara at a park entrance. The sign says,
"No Jews Allowed." (Sugihara Family; Eric Saul, Curator)

In 1941, Sugihara was assigned to the Japanese Consulate in Königsberg, Germany. (Sugihara Family; Eric Saul, Curator)

The Sugihara family in Berlin in 1940. (Sugihara Family; Eric Saul, Curator)

NN.	NATIONALITY	NAME	ENTRANCE or TRANSIT	DATE of TIME	SASHOOKIO	BIXOO
237	POLNISCH	Chil KESTENBERG	TRANSIT	30/VII	2	
238	"	Josef OSKROMSKY	"	"	2	
239	"	Girsch KLEMENTOWSKY	"	"	2	
240	"	Moses GUTMAN	"	"	2	
241	"	Abram STEIN	"	"	2	
242	"	Uehuda LINDWASER	"	"	2	
243	"	Leib MANN	"	"	2	
244	"	Anatol HUFNAGEL	"	"	2	
245	"	Syma OBERMAN	"	"	2	
246	"	Julian GLASS	"	"	2	
247	"	Schabse STEIN	"	"	2	
248	"	Josef ALENBERG	"	"	2	
249	"	Chaim SZLADOWSKI	"	"	2	
250	"	Regina WOPSI	"	"	2	
251	"	Isak WOPSI	"	"	2	
252	"	Jan SPILREIM	"	"	2	
253	"	Aron KOHN	"	"	2	
254	"	Josef PRYWIN	"	"	2	
255	"	Moses STEIN	"	"	2	
256	"	Israel OBERMAN	"	"	2	
257	"	Leon FEIT	"	"	2	
258	"	Alice KRUKOWSKA	"	"	2	
259	"	Ginga MILGROM	"	"	2	
260	"	Szimin BERNSTEIN	"	"	2	
261	"	Kaspel TAUSK	"	"	2	
262	"	Abram TAUSK	"	"	2	
263	"	Icek LEDERMAN	"	"	2	
264	"	Bernhard STEIN	"	"	2	
265	"	Wigdor SPIRO	"	"	2	
266	"	Bencion TOROWITSCH	"	"	2	
267	"	Jankel WAISFELD	"	"	2	
268	"	Julasz SCHLEICHER	"	"	2	
269	"	Felicia MUNZ	"	"	2	
270	"	Rudolf MUNZ	"	"	2	
271	"	Sara GRAFF	"	"	2	
272	"	Ignacy GRAFF	"	"	2	
273	"	Abram FUKIELAN	"	"	2	
274	"	Fain Lejzor MORDKOWICZ	"	"	2	
275	"	Frenkiel Benjamin-Wolf	"	"	2	
276	"	Frenkiel Majer-Szachne	"	"	2	
277	"	Michal GRYNSZTEIN	"	"	2	
278	"	Samson GORDON	"	"	2	
279	"	Rozalia GORDON	"	"	2	
280	"	Adam BRZEZINSKI	"	"	2	
281	"	Szepsel GORDON	"	"	2	
282	"	Perla FRENKIEL	"	"	2	
283	"	Ruwin GRYNSZTEJN	"	"	2	
284	"	Chaim GRYNSZTEJN	"	"	2	
285	"	Szymon FELDBLUM	"	"	2	
286	"	Roza FELDBLUM	"	"	2	
287	Lithuanien	Jankielis ZIMONAS	"	"	2	
288	Polnisch	Marek SZPIGELMAN	"	"	2	
289	"	Isak SSPIGELMAN	"	"	2	
290	"	Maks Ginzberg	"	"	2	
291	"	Nikodem KOW	"	"	2	
292	"	Irena KOW	"	"	2	
293	"	Chawa SZMARAGD	"	"	2	
294	"	Czarna FEFER	"	"	2	
295	"	Marian PRZELOMSKI	"	"	2	
296	"	Edward Krukowski	?	"	2	
297	"	Mortcha BIRENBAUM	?	"	2	
298	"	Walter DEUTSCH	"	"	2	
299	"	Salomon-Boruch-Szmul	"	"	2	
300	"	Matan FLANCREJCH	"	"	2	
301	"	Aleksandr SZTEJNBERG	"	"	2	
302	"	Szmul-Elias TAUB	"	"	2	
303	"	Mieczyslaw KAWA	?	"	2	
304	"	Henryk HARENBERG	"	"	2	
305	"	Wladyslaw LICHTENBAUM	"	"	2	
306	"	Mieczyslaw LICHTENBAUM	"	"	2	
307	"	Izrael SPIRA	"	"	2	

A partial list of the more than 2,193 visas that Sugihara issued, some for individuals, some for families. (Courtesy of Simon Wiesenthal Center Library and Archives, Los Angeles, California, and in memory of George Kadish)

Solly Ganor (center) selling his mother's bread in the Kovno Ghetto. (Courtesy of Simon Wiesenthal Center Library and Archives, Los Angeles, California, and in memory of George Kadish)

An emotional farewell in the Kovno Ghetto. (Courtesy of Simon Wiesenthal Center Library and Archives, Los Angeles, California, and in memory of George Kadish)

Weakened by the harsh internment camps after the war, Haruki Sugihara died in 1947. (Sugihara Family; Eric Saul, Curator)

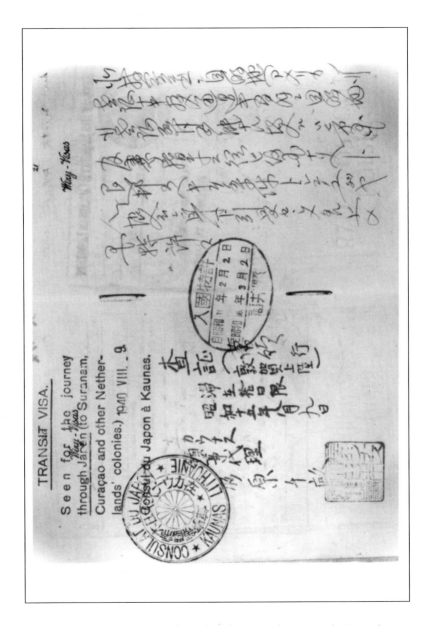

One of the visas issued by Sugihara. (Sugihara Family; Eric Saul, Curator)

Chiune Sugihara's visas saved the lives of thousands of Jewish refugees. It was one of the largest rescues of Jews in the Holocaust.

the Jewish community. Many refugees were living in the streets or at the railway station. Their only food was given to them at communal soup kitchens set up by charities.

But one day, all refugees, rich and poor, perked up. A thrilling rumor of a possible source of escape had suddenly begun to circulate.

Outside 30 Vaizgantas Street, birds sang at dawn. Since Sugihara always woke early, Yukiko also woke. This way she could eat breakfast with her husband, after he'd worked in his garden, but before the children woke. After breakfast, Chiune would go downstairs and begin his work at the consulate. This was the daily routine.

One morning after breakfast, on July 27, 1940, Yukiko was reading and enjoying the sun, which had begun to pour into the sitting room through the curtains. Chiune unexpectedly returned after he had begun work. He was agitated. He urged her to look out the window.

Yukiko went with him to the window and pulled aside the curtain, expecting to see the gate and the empty, silent street. Instead, directly below was a crowd of people milling behind the gate, and an uneven line had formed around the consulate. She observed that many of these people had desperate looks on their faces, were filthy, and were agitated.

When she turned her disturbed eyes toward her husband, Sugihara told her that he'd sent Borislav out to get information. Yukiko let go of the curtain, but the image of the anxious faces on the street below had seared itself into both of their minds.

CHAPTER

13

Borislav *returned and reported* that there were more than one hundred Jewish people outside, that thousands more could be expected here in the next few days. Sugihara wondered what they wanted from him. He hoped for an answer soon, because his staff had arrived at the consulate and a meeting was about to begin.

Upstairs, Yukiko again peeked at the scene below. She tried not to be seen, but someone down below must have spotted her, because suddenly voices shouted up at her. She saw arms reach up in her direction. A few men were even trying to climb over the consulate fence, while others were trying to restrain them.

Setsuko, Yukiko's sister, walked up behind Yukiko and looked out the window. She found the scene so astonishing that she got a camera and took several photographs.

After the staff meeting, Sugihara wrote down what was wanted of him in his notebook: *These people had walked for many days under severe conditions, dragging themselves on painful feet and enduring countless hardships. Their objective was to reach Kaunas. What they wanted was, somehow, for the Japanese Consulate to issue transit visas that would allow them to travel through the Soviet Union in order to escape the Nazis.*

A rumor had spread like wildfire that the Dutch Consulate might be willing to issue visas to Curaçao, a small colony in the West Indies belonging to Holland. If there was a way to travel through the Soviet Union to the international port of Vladivostok in eastern Russia, then get to Japan, the refugees had a chance of getting transport to Curaçao, or even to Shanghai where Jews didn't need a visa.

That's why they'd come. In the hope of getting visas from the Japanese consul.

Upstairs, Yukiko stared out the window as the crowd grew larger and noisier. She worried about her husband. She was feeling quite upset.

Downstairs in the consulate office, Sugihara sat at

his desk and anguished about the hunted people who were gathered outside his gate, the same sad people who'd concerned him when he was driving in the countryside and saw them along the roads. There was no question that human beings were asking for help. His help. Help which he doubted that his superiors would be willing to allow him to give.

14

When the children awoke they, too, looked out the window and saw children like themselves in the crowd below. Hiroki was worried. He asked his mother what they wanted.

Chiaki, although only three years old, was also upset. Yukiko held the new baby in her arms. She tried to explain to the children that the people below had come to ask their father for help, that these people were in danger of being killed by bad men.

When Sugihara came upstairs, Hiroki begged his father to please help the poor little children. Sugihara explained that because of the restless crowd in front of the consulate, the children would not be able to go outside and play in the park. As Sugihara and his wife and children looked through the window, several more men tried to climb over the fence.

Chiune sent Borislav and Gudze outside to try to bring order to the crowd. It was so chaotic that when the maid left to do the grocery shopping, people tried to push into the building. She was so frightened, she scurried back inside to safety. Gudze and Borislav physically pushed the crowd away and struggled to shut the wrought iron gate. If some order wasn't brought to the crowd, it would overrun the consulate before too long, as even more people were arriving.

Mr. Sugihara decided that he would speak with a committee of refugees. Five men were chosen from the crowd to represent everyone. As soon as the committee was chosen, the crowd calmed down.

The committee was headed by a Pole named Zorach Warhaftig. Another member, named Izzy Graudenz, was a rabbi traveling with an entire religious school. Rabbi Graudenz was originally from Germany. Another committee member was named Yehoshua Nishri.

The committee sat tensely in the consul's office. One by one, the men spoke and Sugihara sat silently and gave them his complete attention.

Warhaftig spread out a map. He explained that he and the others were desperate. All of them had narrowly escaped to Kaunas. They'd come to the Japanese consulate because they'd heard that they might be able to get transit visas which would permit them to travel through Japan and escape from the Nazis who hunted them. They were now officially asking the Japanese consul to issue these visas.

Chiune listened to each gruesome story of escape, and to their pleas. After all the men had spoken, Mr. Sugihara explained that of course he could issue a few visas by his own authority, but he could not possibly issue hundreds or even thousands of visas. For that he would need permission from the Ministry of Foreign Affairs in Japan. He told the assembled committee that he needed time to think. He suggested that they meet again the next day.

When they'd gone, he sat alone in his office. He remembered a Japanese proverb he'd learned in school. The proverb said: *Even the hunter cannot kill a bird that comes to him for refuge.* But what could he do?

Because the maid wasn't able to go out and shop, there was no smell of fresh food cooking. Later in the day Chiune took Yukiko aside. He showed her a letter that he'd just received from the Soviet government. It contained instructions that he close the Japanese consulate in the first week of August.

All night, Chiune and Yukiko couldn't sleep and thrashed and tossed in bed.

Below, in the street, the crowd continued to grow. Whole families were sleeping on the sidewalk now. Some refugees just stood staring up at the darkened windows of the consulate all night.

15

First thing in the morning, Sugihara called another meeting with the five representatives and invited Mr. Jan Zwartendijk, the acting Dutch consul. Quickly, discussion began concerning Curaçao. Sugihara asked Zwartendijk if there was even a landing location on the tiny island of Curaçao.

Mr. Zwartendijk couldn't help smiling. He replied that he doubted that there were even any customs officials in Curaçao. The committee members laughed, a much needed moment of levity in an otherwise tense meeting that was a matter of life and death.

Mr. Zwartendijk told the assembled that he *was* willing to help them. All eyes turned toward Sugihara then. Mr. Sugihara met their eyes. He announced that if his wife agreed, he would draft a cable to his Foreign Ministry asking permission to issue visas.

The committee left with their first ray of hope. They agreed to return when Mr. Sugihara was ready to finalize his answer.

That evening Chiune sat with Yukiko and told her that he planned to cable the Ministry of Foreign Affairs about the refugee situation, but he needed Yukiko's help now in order to make a decision. He leaned closer to his wife and asked her what she thought.

Without a moment's pause, Yukiko told him that she agreed with him. She felt that Chiune *should* help these desperate people if he could.

No more words were exchanged.

Yukiko accompanied Chiune into the office. They shut the door and turned on the light. Chiune began the complicated process of sending a cable to the Japanese Foreign Minister. He drafted it using diplomatic codes. Then Yukiko carefully rewrote the cable by hand in triplicate.

The uncoded cable stated:

I request permission to issue visas to hundreds of Jewish people who have come to the consulate here in Kaunas seeking transit visas. They are suffering extremely. As a fellow human being, I cannot refuse their requests. Please permit me to issue visas to them. This request is a humanitarian plea. The refugees' request for visas should not be denied.

The first copy of the cable was sent to the Japanese ambassador in Germany. Number two went to the Japanese ambassador in nearby Latvia. The final cable went to Sugihara's superior, Foreign Minister Yosuke Matsouka in Tokyo.

Then the waiting began. As they waited, more arriving refugees crowded the sidewalk in front of the consulate.

CHAPTER

16

Two days later, a reply was received. It read:

> Concerning transit visas requested previously STOP. Advise
> absolutely not to be issued to any traveler not holding firm
> end visa with guaranteed departure ex Japan STOP. No
> exceptions STOP. No further inquiries expected STOP.
> K. Tanaka Foreign Ministry Tokyo.

Sugihara digested the information. He decided to immediately send another cable.

The tense waiting continued. It was taking a toll on the crowd. Their faces were gray and pathetic. Many had no food and were afraid of losing their place on line by going to the soup kitchen. Yukiko and Chiune were weak from lack of sleep.

At night Chiune voiced all his doubts to Yukiko. He pondered whether or not they should shut the consulate as he'd been ordered and abandon the entire situation. Should they leave the refugees to the whims of fate?

Yukiko's skeptical look told her husband what he already knew, that he wouldn't do such a thing. It was not in his nature. Chiune squeezed his wife's hand. Of course, she was right.

Finally a reply came to the second cable:

Permission denied. The Japanese Department of the Interior feels that such an action would endanger public security. The shipping company that operates the ferryboats between Vladivostok and the Port of Tsuruga also rejects this request, the reason being that such an action would compromise passenger safety.

Chiune showed Yukiko the reply. His face was drawn, his jaw clenched. Sometimes you had to ask several times in Japan, so he sent a third and final cable. The waiting continued.

He was alone in his office when the coded reply arrived. Again, permission was denied.

For a long time Mr. Sugihara sat silently in his office with the third cable. He remembered the code of conduct he and all schoolchildren had been taught: (a) *Do not be a burden to others*; (b) *Take care of others*; (c) *Do not expect rewards for your goodness*. He remembered the Jewish refugees he'd seen in Harbin long ago, threadbare and haunted people, walking toward the railway station with flimsy suitcases in hand hoping to escape the unjust anti-Semitism that shadowed their lives.

He looked out the window at the crowd below. Yet another young man had come to his home for protection. Was he dangerous? No. Was he a spy? No. Was he a traitor? No. He was just a Jewish teenager who wanted to live.

Finally Sugihara faced Yukiko. He told her he had decided to issue visas in defiance of his Foreign Ministry, under his own authority as consul. He asked if she approved of his decision.

Her answer was yes.

He warned her that he didn't know what would happen to them after such an act.

She repeated her answer.

Mr. Sugihara gathered the rest of his family together; his sister-in-law, Setsuko, his three sons. He told them what he was going to do. He explained that

67

if he signed all the visas, he must be prepared to be dismissed by the Foreign Ministry.

By acting against his own government, he would most likely lose all chance of advancement, ruin his career, and be disgraced. He might endanger all their lives. He added that although he might have to disobey his government, if he didn't act, he would be disobeying God.

The entire family agreed that he should help the refugees, even if it meant risking their future, or their lives. Even the baby, Haruki, their Bright Spirit, seemed to be listening and was in accord with his brothers.

CHAPTER
17

Early the following morning, Sugihara went through the door leading into the garage. He and his chauffeur got into the car. Then, the moving car gently nudged aside the crowd of refugees, whose number had gone from hundreds to more like a thousand. The chauffeur drove directly to the Soviet embassy.

Sugihara met with the Soviet consul. The meeting got off to a good start because the consul was awed by Chiune's ability to speak excellent Russian. Chiune knew that the love of the Russian language meant a lot to Russians. He carefully explained his mission, that he needed permission for a large number of refugees to traverse Russia — to cross Siberia and be permitted on boats between Vladivostok and Tsuruga — to get to Japan.

After a brief negotiation, the Japanese consul persuaded the Soviet consul to agree to let the refugees pass through Russia and to board ships at the ports.

Outside the consulate, the frustrated crowd was at the end of its endurance. When the shiny Buick with the Japanese flag on the front hood edged through their midst, the set face of the consul was unreadable. Their worst fear seemed about to come to pass, that this consulate — like all the others — would turn its back on them. And then, since there seemed to be absolutely no other ray of hope, they would be like hunted animals who had been chased into the trap, and the trap door would close.

18

Because the temperature had dropped during the night, many people who stood outside the Japanese Consulate had gotten chills, and they were numb with fear and exhaustion. When the Japanese consul stepped outside and stood in front of his gate asking for attention, he did it so unobtrusively that it took a minute for his presence to sink in. When it did, every eye was riveted on his face.

In a soft but authoritative voice, he announced that he would issue visas to each and every one of the people in line, to the last man, woman, and child.

Watching him from behind the curtain, Yukiko heard him make his statement to the crowd. The crowd acted stunned at first, then it seemed like an electric shock jolted every person. They all surged toward her husband, looking as if they might crush him with joy. She felt a deep sense of gladness.

Strangers hugged each other. People kissed. Families and friends squeezed and pounded each other with relief. Hands raised up pointing to heaven. Some people couldn't stop the tears and collapsed against each other sobbing loudly. The crowd's force pushed Sugihara against the garage door. He held his hands up, signaling that they back off.

The elated Jewish refugees did not realize that Sugihara was disobeying orders from his superiors at the Foreign Ministry and in the Japanese government. It was a secret. They had no idea he was risking everything.

Sugihara conferred with Borislav, then turned away and walked back inside, while Borislav wrote out numbered cards that he began to distribute to people in order of their place in line.

Chiune sat down with Yukiko and drank several cups of strong coffee.

That very day, the consulate organized into a kind of factory for visas. One by one, Sugihara interviewed each refugee. He quietly asked questions — name, age, number of individuals in each family, country of origin, country of destination, port of entry, permit for country of destination, source of funds.

Finally he placed the official stamp of Japan and the Emperor on the visa and handwritten information, finalizing the document with his signature. Before he put the visa into the refugee's hand, he took a moment to look at each person with his warm, dark eyes and wish him good luck.

It was slow work because Sugihara had to fill out each visa in longhand and also keep a log of the visa numbers issued, including the name of the recipient or family.

Because the refugees found it hard to pronounce his first name — Chiune — he told them to call him *Sempo*.

It was late morning by the time No. 22 entered. His name was Ludvik Salomon; he was from Cracow, Poland and had arduously traveled across the Carpathian Mountains. Days before, Salomon had been spooning hot soup into his mouth at the Café Metropole, and grumbling about the difficulties of escape when someone had mentioned the Japanese consul. Salomon had dropped his soup spoon and raced over to Vaizgantas Street and was among the very first in line. Despite hunger pangs, Salomon hadn't budged for many days.

Sugihara offered Salomon a cup of tea while he studied his passport and began filling out the required visa and information. Salomon held his breath until he saw that the final signature had been penned.

By lunchtime Chiune's hands ached from hours of writing. Yukiko looked down from the stairway to see if he was coming up for lunch. Shortly, the maid came to report to her that he would not be stopping for lunch.

Sugihara's employee — Wolfgang Gudze, the German — and other staff assisted him. They collected information and stamped official seals on the visas and passports.

Late in the afternoon, Chiune called to Yukiko to ask how many people were left outside. Yukiko looked out through the curtain. Her heart sank when she saw that the line was longer than ever and more people were dashing down the street to join.

She called down to tell him there were many left.

Yukiko was afraid to tell him just how many.

19

From then on, the consulate opened its doors at eight in the morning and remained open late into the night. Chiune hoped to write and issue three hundred visas each day. He then received a second letter from the Soviets ordering that he shut down the consulate. Pressure increased when, on August 2, Sugihara received a cable with official orders from the Japanese Foreign Ministry to shut down the Japanese Consulate in Kaunas. Immediately.

Sugihara made an official, passionate request to the Soviet Embassy for an extension. They officially responded that they would consider his request and inform him when they'd made their decision. He knew that if they refused, he would have to quickly shut his door and stop issuing visas.

Fearful that his request would be refused, Sugihara wrote out and signed visa after visa as quickly as he could. He issued one to Amalia Strich, a pretty young woman who, the previous winter, had skied across the mountains to the border of Lithuania. At the border, she had crossed on a sled. The driver of the sled told the guard at the border that Amalia was his wife and they were on their way to church.

Once inside Lithuania, Amalia had gone to Vilna. Although she was trained in mathematics, she took lessons in cosmetics in order to have a practical way of earning money. When she heard about the Japanese consul, she hurried to Kaunas by train. Sugihara gave Amalia a precious visa.

A German Jew from Frankfurt named Moshe Zupnik had been waiting in line for days. Zupnik was a very young man. He was holding three hundred passports and other travel documents that belonged to the entire Mir Yeshiva, a famous Jewish religious school in Poland. The Yeshiva consisted of teachers, students, and their families. Finally, Zupnik's number was called and he was shown into the consulate.

Sugihara was busy, so Zupnik first spoke with Wolfgang Gudze. Gudze asked him who he was.

Zupnik replied that he was a member of the Mir Yeshiva and had three hundred passports with him. He hoped that the entire school could all go to Curaçao together. Gudze gasped when he heard three hundred passports! He shook his head to say that the consul would never allow it.

Zupnik pleaded to be allowed to talk to the consul himself. Gudze stared hard at Zupnik, then left the room. Zupnik heard Gudze reporting that a man had come with three hundred passports, what should he do?

When Gudze returned he told Zupnik that the consul was coming right in to speak with him. Within a few minutes Sugihara entered the room, walked directly toward Zupnik, and asked who he was. Zupnik explained that he and the others were a rabbinical seminary with over three hundred people who wanted to go to Curaçao.

Sugihara looked perplexed. He examined the pile of passports. Then he told Gudze that it was all right.

Gudze asked how he could handle such a crowd.

Zupnik offered to help. Sugihara told Gudze that Zupnik would help him and Sugihara went back into his office.

A chair was pulled up in the corridor and Zupnik was seated next to Gudze. Sugihara would write by hand in his office, Gudze and Zupnik would stamp.

Once, Zupnik looked up and saw a beautiful woman standing nervously at the top of the stairway. She was wearing a kimono and holding a crying infant.

The Zielonka family were rich grain brokers and had jewelry and gold coins sewn into the lining of their coats. They got visas for the entire family.

A pretty, earnest woman named Zelda Bernstein was issued a visa.

Next came Chaya Liba Szepsenwol, who was sixteen. She was very poor. She and her sister, Fejga, were called in to speak with Sugihara. They were so scared that they were shaking. Sugihara asked where their parents were.

Chaya told him that their father was not living and their mother had no papers. He looked at them with sympathy and began writing out a visa. Fejga and Chaya started to cry. They kept saying, "*Dziekuje, dziekuje, dziekuje,*" "thank you" in Polish.

The consulate was closing for the day. When the Szepsenwol sisters came out through the garage door, some people — whose turn wouldn't come for another day or more — were angry and jeered at them. However, other people on line who saw them clutching the precious documents, shaking and sobbing, patted their heads and shouted, "Good luck. God be with you."

CHAPTER

20

The summer in Kaunas grew hot and humid. A thunderstorm rolled across the city, then passed on.

One afternoon, the refugee who had briefly stayed with Solly Ganor's family the previous winter, Mr. Rosenblat, along with his little daughter, knocked on the Ganors' door. Beside Rosenblat stood a young man who wore the black coat and hat and had the beard and earlocks of an Orthodox Jewish man.

Chaim Ganor received them. Mr. Rosenblat introduced the boy as a student from the Telzer Yeshiva. Excitedly, Rosenblat explained that Mr. Sugihara was issuing visas through Russia and Japan to Dutch Curaçao. They had come to ask Chaim a favor. Because he knew Mr. Sugihara, would he go with them and remind Mr. Sugihara of their desperate situation? Getting transit visas from him was certainly their only hope.

Mr. Ganor agreed to do what he could and made an appointment with the consul.

First thing in the morning, Chaim, Solly, Lea, Mr. Rosenblat, and the Yeshiva student walked across town to the Japanese consulate.

The Sugihara that greeted them was not the same man that had given Solly stamps months before. Now, Mr. Sugihara looked exhausted, tense, and had dark circles under his eyes. He was in rumpled shirtsleeves. Sugihara invited them into his office and sat them down as Mr. Ganor explained why they had come. Immediately Mr. Sugihara wrote out visas on the passports of Rosenblat, Lea, and the student, and also on the Ganor passports that Chaim had brought.

Rosenblat burst into tears. He bent and kissed Sugihara's hands. He told Sugihara that he was privileged to stand in front of a true humanitarian. Sugihara looked directly at Chaim and suggested that his family, too, leave Lithuania.

Mr. Ganor lowered his gaze. He explained that when he'd sold his business and had money to care for his family abroad, then perhaps he'd consider leaving. But not before.

Mr. Sugihara felt deep concern for these friends, the Ganors. He reached into his desk drawer and took out an envelope and handed it to Solly.

Solly opened the envelope and was pleased to see another batch of Japanese stamps. He thanked Sempo Sugihara profusely. Sugihara shook Solly's hand. *"Vaya con Dios,"* he said to Solly. Then Sugihara showed Solly and Chaim and the others out, looked sadly at them one last time, and closed the door.

Solly asked his father what *"Vaya con Dios"* meant. Chaim told him that it meant "Go with God" in Spanish.

But why had he said it in Spanish? Solly wondered. Mr. Ganor shook his head. Mr. Sugihara was a puzzling person; all Solly's father could say for sure was that Mr. Sugihara had spoken from his heart.

21

After the consulate door closed for the day, Sugihara put his pen down and went right up to bed. Although he'd missed two meals that day, he had no interest in food. Totally exhausted, he closed his eyes.

Yukiko sat down beside him and began to massage his hands and arms. Although her hands were delicate and small, they were surprisingly strong. Long after Chiune had fallen asleep, Yukiko continued massaging his cramped, aching palms.

In days to come, on awakening, Yukiko would peek out from behind the curtain and look down at the street below. Sugihara would ask her how many people were left outside.

Each time she'd reply that there were many, afraid to say just *how* many.

Every day Chiune went back to his desk and began writing. Time was running out. The Russians hadn't responded to his request for an extension. Also, the cable from the Japanese government ordering him to shut the consulate was always in the back of his mind.

The days passed laboriously. He handwrote hundreds of visas each day.

One day, Chiune's ink began to run out. Rather than stop writing while he waited for more ink, he watered down the existing ink. Then, he had to press down harder on the pen. He pressed so hard that the pen snapped in two.

Chiune's bloodshot eyes were ringed with darker and darker circles, his usually neat hair was disheveled. The line of anxious and desperate people still snaked along the curb of Vaizgantas Street and around the block, continually lengthening.

The second week in August arrived all too quickly. Sugihara was overdue to shut down the consulate as ordered by both the Soviets and his own government.

On August 10, first thing in the morning, Sugihara looked down at the crowd from the window. He later wrote about the sight that day: *There were not only male* refugees, among them were women, old people and children. They all seemed very tired and exhausted. I did not know whether they had any place to sleep in Kaunas, maybe they just slept in the station or on the street.

The more affluent and better-connected refugees who had gotten to the Japanese consulate before anyone else had now mostly disappeared with their precious visas. The new people who squatted in line, or stared up at his window, seemed poorer, more miserable and pathetic. These people had spent many months either foraging for food or living off soup and bread in the charity kitchens set up by the Lithuanian Jewish community.

That day, Chiune dressed and went down to his office. Before the consulate opened, he told his staff that he had decided — with whatever time was left — to loosen the rules. From now on, whether the documentation warranted it or not, he would grant visas to anyone and everyone. Also, on that day, he stopped keeping a log of the visas that he wrote.

Thus began, with the ticking clock in the background, even more frantic work for Chiune and his helpers. Many of the new refugees on line had forged documents, many had Polish passports that were too old, or many had suspect Czechoslovakian passports.

Some had no documents at all. Now it no longer mattered to the Japanese consul what they had.

People waiting in line discussed Consul Sugihara; one refugee commented that he was a *mensch*, which in Yiddish means a man of worth and dignity. Another refugee disagreed, calling him Elijah the Prophet, whom God sends in time of trouble in one disguise or another. This time, God had sent Elijah disguised as a Japanese diplomat!

22

On a cool morning in mid-August a letter was delivered from the Russian Embassy. Chiune's hand trembled as he slit it open with a sharp letter opener. He began to read. His helpers tensely watched him. Had time finally run out?

Chiune let out his breath. He pushed the letter over for Gudze to read and told Gudze to make the announcement.

Gudze went out front. He got the attention of the crowd and told them that the Soviet government had issued the Japanese Consulate an extension. Rather than the previous order to shut down immediately, they now had permission to remain open until the end of August. Until August 28, to be exact!

The relief of the crowd was immediate and exhilarating. Tears sprang to some eyes. A murmur of hope rippled through the line of waiting people, around the corner, and down the street.

Inside, Chiune continued to write and write, and his staff to stamp and stamp all day, knowing they would work into the night.

Late in the day, exhausted, Chiune went upstairs to see Yukiko. It seemed as though he didn't have the energy to write one more word. So, Yukiko began to massage his hands. She knew that prolonged fatigue was showing through, but she encouraged him to issue more visas and save as many lives as he could.

He smiled at his supportive wife who, whenever he needed it, gave him encouragement to go on. He sat with her and let her massage his hands. Finally he stood up and leaned against the windowsill. He looked down at the crowd below just as Solly Ganor walked past the consulate. As Mr. Sugihara waved down at Solly with a smile, Solly waved back at Sempo Sugihara.

Downstairs, in the corridor, Gudze and Zupnik sat at their table and stamped visa after visa. They'd been sitting like this — side by side — for almost two weeks. One was a Jew, the other a German, but they were working together. Zupnik asked Gudze what he'd do when the consulate closed. Gudze told him that he'd go back to the fatherland to fight for Germany.

Had he supported Hitler? Zupnik wanted to know. Gudze explained that at one point he had been against Hitler, but now Hitler was the leader of all of the Germans and, yes, Gudze supported him.

But, Hitler hates Jews! Zupnik exclaimed, asking if Gudze, too, hated Jews. Gudze told him that he didn't hate Jews. He had gained respect for Jews, particularly religious ones. In fact, he confided, before he'd married his German wife, he'd had a connection with a Jewish girl. He hadn't married her, but since then, he had respect for Jews.

Was his wife in Kaunas? She was; she was a teacher. Zupnik couldn't resist, and asked intimately why Gudze was helping Jewish people now. Gudze admitted that he had pity for them. They wanted to get out of Hitler's way, so he'd helped them get their visas.

Just then, Sugihara came back downstairs to his office. They could see from his face that some of the fatigue had lifted, that he had gotten a second wind. He was ready to handwrite the next batch of visas and work into the night.

*   *   *

Far away in England, in late summer of 1940, bombs were falling. Italy was preparing an assault on North Africa. All over occupied Europe, hardship and terror were increasing and a noose was tightening around every single Jewish neck.

CHAPTER
23

While Sugihara and his staff wrote and stamped, Yukiko either stood at the top of the stairway or watched the crowd through the window. She wrote one of her short poems called a *tanka*:

> There in the crowd
> *Waiting for visas*
> *Is a boy*
> *Clutching his father ever so tightly*
> *His face is dirty*

She had offered to help Chiune write visas, but he'd told her that it might be too dangerous for her to do any actual writing. If he alone wrote, then he could bear sole responsibility. In fact, he requested that she and the children stay out of the office entirely.

Chiune received a final warning from the Japanese government. The telegram insisted that Sugihara immediately close the consulate in Lithuania and report to Berlin.

Sugihara gravely read this telegram. The time had come, but nonetheless he continued to write visas while taking the preliminary actions necessary to close and abandon the Japanese Consulate. He told Yukiko to begin to pack and prepare for departure. He told Wolfgang Gudze to make preparations, too. He told Zupnik that his help was no longer needed.

Zupnik gathered his things together. When Zupnik stood up, Gudze realized that Zupnik — who had sat beside him for at least fourteen days stamping visas — was hardly older than a teenage boy.

Zupnik asked Gudze how he could thank him. Gudze looked steely-eyed at Zupnik and told him to remember that the world was like a *rad*. *Rad* was the German word for wheel. Gudze explained that whoever is on top today, might be down tomorrow. He asked Zupnik not to forget what he had done for him and the others, and said good-bye.

Sugihara was sitting at his desk when Zupnik came to the door to say good-bye. Sugihara was writing a visa for an old Polish man and woman. He dated it August 28, 1940. Then he handed it over and said, "*Zeit gezunt*," which means "Be well" in Yiddish.

The woman knelt down, bowed low, and kissed Sugihara's feet. When she stood up, her eyes were soaking wet.

Zupnik said good-bye to Sugihara. Sugihara thanked him for his help, gripped him firmly by the shoulder, and wished him good luck!

24

Late at night, on the very last night that they would spend at 30 Vaizgantas, Yukiko finished the last of the packing. Suddenly, she smelled the acrid odor of smoke.

She ran downstairs. She saw smoke pouring out from under the closed door of his office. She hit the door with her fist, shouting, "Chiune! Chiune!"

He opened the door. He told her wryly not to worry, he was just putting some papers in order. She looked in and saw documents roasting, sizzling, and curling up in a small fire he'd built. She felt relieved, shut the door, and went back upstairs.

The next day, the bags were packed and lined up in

the foyer. The furniture was covered with sheets. The seal of the consulate and other high security papers had already been sent to Berlin.

Yukiko, Setsuko, and the three children squeezed into the car. Then Mr. Sugihara came outside carrying his briefcase. He glanced sadly at his garden, which was overgrown with weeds because of neglect. He went to the gate and put up a sign. Then he, too, climbed into the Buick.

As the car drove along the street, Yukiko saw the line of people watching them. She saw terrible despair on their faces as the car passed. She ached to apologize to them, to ask their forgiveness for leaving them behind. Tears welled up, but she was silent. So was Sugihara.

The sign that Sugihara left on the gate of the empty consulate informed the refugees that the Japanese consul would be staying at the Hotel Metropolis in Kaunas. The car drove through the city. Above them on the hill was the Ninth Fort, a crumbling fortress built in the 1800s. They passed Konrad's Café on Osios Vasario Street. They passed the place where it was said that Napoleon had fallen from his horse on his way to attack Russia in 1812.

The car stopped at the Hotel Metropolis. The Sugiharas registered at the hotel. Chiune was frightfully drained, but as soon as he entered the room, a message was sent to tell him that he was wanted down in the lobby.

He dragged himself back down to the lobby. Already, a group of refugees had made a ragtag line through the hotel lobby. Their faces showed their desperation. Instead of resting, Chiune began to handwrite visas for these people. Although he no longer had the consul seal or the official stamps, he wrote on official paper.

In his heart, Chiune didn't know if these papers would be honored by officials, but he wrote anyway. He suggested to some of these refugees that they say, "*Banzai, Nippon!*" to any Japanese immigration officials that they met, when and if they got to Japan. Perhaps this would make the officials more sympathetic to them.

Someone asked him what the words meant.

It meant "Long live Japan!"

Even when Yukiko came down and begged him to come upstairs and at least rest for a little while, he continued to write.

25

They *stayed at the Hotel Metropolis* for several days. The entire time, Chiune sat in a stuffed chair in the lobby of the hotel handwriting visas and handing them to individuals or families. No matter how many he wrote, the line of waiting people grew longer. Their faces were imploring. Finally Yukiko tapped him on the shoulder and told him that they had to go to the train.

The crowd of waiting refugees stood helplessly. Their eyes showed the terror they were experiencing at the sight of the Japanese consul's departure. Mr. Sugihara begged the people remaining to please forgive him. He simply couldn't write anymore. He wished each of them the best. He began to walk away, then turned back and faced the frozen refugees. He bowed deeply before them.

As the diplomatic Buick with the flapping Japanese flag on the hood drove the Sugihara family and their baggage to the railway station, the crowd of refugees followed, wending their way through the streets of Kaunas.

The Sugihara family boarded the train. The swarm of refugees gathered beside the train. While the train stood in the station, preparing to depart, Mr. Sugihara wrote visas on sheets of paper and passed them out the train window into outstretched hands. He wrote as fast as he could.

Finally the train moved. A voice shouted, "Banzai Nippon!"

Then a chorus of voices shouted, "Banzai Nippon! Banzai Nippon!"

The train gathered speed. Chiune threw a handful of diplomatic stationery out the window to the refugees. One strong voice shouted "Sempo Sugihara!" Others shouted phrases like, "We'll never forget you!" and "We will see you again!"

Some of the stronger people ran beside the train as it sped up. Sugihara let go of the last sheets of diplomatic stationery that were clutched in his hand. They fell soundlessly onto the ringing tracks.

26

Hiroki asked his father if they were going to Berlin. Chiune nodded.

Yukiko looked wanly at the receding outskirts of Kaunas as the train passed into the countryside. She felt terribly sad and feared for the many refugees who had been left standing at the consulate or in the railway station with empty hands. Not far away was the forest of crosses — thousands of them — on the eerie Hill of Crosses.

The train transversed the rivers Niemunas and Neris and passed the ruins of an old castle. But Sugihara saw nothing of the late summer countryside; he fell into a deep and heavy sleep that lasted almost the entire journey to Berlin.

When the train pulled into the grand Berlin train station, which was festooned with Nazi eagles, the Sugiharas were met in proper diplomatic fashion. Sugihara was deeply worried about the visas that he'd issued in Kaunas. He feared that he would be punished, but hid his anxiety behind his seemingly calm face.

They were driven to their hotel along green tree-lined avenues that were quite wide. Black-and-red swastika flags flew from windows and flagpoles, flapping in the breeze, celebrating the continuous string of Hitler's victories.

Safely inside their room at the hotel, both Yukiko and Chiune remained troubled. They could not forget the sight of the refugees left standing empty-handed and frozen at the station. Yukiko wrote another *tanka*:

> The train pulls away,
> hands reaching out the window
> Passing out visas
> Hands reaching towards the windows
> for visas for life —
> Hope

When she expressed to Chiune her haunting sad-ness about the refugees, he told her that he'd left instructions for refugees to try to get visas at the Japanese Embassy in Moscow. Perhaps there was still hope, even for those who remained at the train station.

In Berlin, Chiune and Yukiko waited for the ax to fall. What would the Japanese Ministry do about the thousands of visas Chiune had issued to enemies of Hitler? The first meeting Sugihara had was with Foreign Minister Kurusu. Kurusu was the most important Japanese representative in Europe.

Late in the afternoon, when Chiune returned to their hotel room after his meeting, the first thing he told Yukiko was that Minister Kurusu hadn't said anything to him about the visas.

Yukiko's apprehension lifted.

Then Chiune added that Consul General Ichige had been ordered back to Japan and would shortly be vacating his post in Prague, and that he, Sugihara, had been recommended to replace Ichige in Prague.

Yukiko liked the idea of Prague, a city of history and music. But Sugihara suggested that she not get too excited since he suspected that this posting might not last very long.

27

They arrived in Prague, Czechoslovakia, by train. The consulate was an old, rococo building on the Moldau River. The interior was luxuriously furnished and had a grand crystal chandelier. Several rooms were lined with Japanese silk, one contained silver decorations, two others contained gold decorations.

A staff was provided — five maids, a cook, and two officers for the consulate. A very sweet young maid named Marnya quickly formed a warm relationship with the children.

As soon as he was settled, Sugihara was ordered to write a report that gave all the details of his work in Kaunas. Part of his responsibility was to list the number of visas that had been stamped by his consulate. Although he delayed sending the information in, regardless of the possible repercussions, he told the truth.

Sugihara's log showed that he'd issued more than 2,193 visas. Some of these visas were for individuals, others were for entire families, so he couldn't accurately account for the total number of individuals who had been given visas. Of course, there was also the problem that he'd stopped keeping a list in early August, so he couldn't add up the total visas given while in Kaunas. He compiled his documents, then sent them to Tokyo.

Chiune and Yukiko worried about what would happen when these papers arrived in Japan. They lived with the anxiety of repercussions for their deeds in Kaunas, but with *gaman*, the Japanese virtue of keeping suffering to oneself.

In late September 1940, Japan and Germany — Hirohito and Hitler — signed an alliance known as the Axis Tripartite Pact, which meant that Berlin, Rome, and Tokyo were now allied.

Prague was a very social city with an active nightlife. It was especially lively for diplomats. There were parties, dinners with fine wine, gourmet food, and dancing. Once again Yukiko dressed in her beautiful kimonos and Sugihara wore elegant evening clothes. Often the diplomatic car drove them back to the consulate quite late. The city was silent except for the beautiful church bells, which could be heard throughout the entire city.

Yukiko began to relax. She started to study the German language, and also to paint on canvas. She liked Prague so much that she painted the sights of the City of One Hundred Spires — the seven bridges that crossed the river, and the gargoyles with pipes protruding from their mouths, high up on St. Vitus Cathedral.

When Sugihara had leisure time in Prague, he took the family for drives out into the countryside once again. They visited pine forests, castles, and forts. The children were getting older and could appreciate the sights much more than before.

One day Sugihara was told that one of Hitler's most important foreign ministers — Joachim von Ribbentrop — was coming to Prague. Sugihara and other diplomats were summoned to a meeting. Sugihara dressed carefully that day.

His car drove through the city toward the meeting. He passed the astronomical clock on Town Hall. On the hour, the figure of Death rang a bell, and was followed by a musician, then a rich man with his money, and finally a vain man with a mirror. Far off, nude giants flanked the gate of the Prague Castle high on a hilltop.

As Chiune approached the room where the meeting was being held, an unpleasant German shepherd dog blocked the door. The dog was tied to the entrance, and growled at each diplomat that passed. Its master, Herr von Ribbentrop, had taken the largest, highest desk in the room. A large photograph of Hitler in uniform making the Nazi salute was on the wall in an ornate frame.

Ribbentrop spoke condescendingly to the assembled diplomats, ordering them all to leave Czechoslovakia immediately. Silence followed this statement. No one had the courage to speak up except Chiune Sugihara, who broke the silence. He stood up and addressed Ribbentrop, asserting that Ribbentrop couldn't just order them to leave.

He said that since the Triple Alliance, Japan was an equal partner with Germany, not to be treated in any subordinate way. Although Hitler had, in his racist, hating way, often called Japanese people "lacquered half-monkeys" they were now his allies. Now it was

Ribbentrop's turn to be silent. He glared at the digni-
fied Japanese diplomat for daring to confront him, but
he was impressed by his courage.

When Chiune returned home, he told Yukiko that
he'd been ordered to Berlin for a meeting.

He returned from Berlin within a very few days. He
informed Yukiko that Ambassador Oshima had in-
structed him to shut the consulate in Prague, and open
one in Königsberg, Germany, near the Russian border.

Noticing the crease in Yukiko's forehead, Chiune
reassured her that the Kaunas visas had not been
brought up in Berlin.

Yukiko was sad at the thought of leaving pleasant
Prague. She asked him when they would leave and he
told her they'd leave in March.

CHAPTER

28

Early one bitter, cold morning in February 1941, Zelda Bernstein woke Masha. Zelda had gotten a visa from the Japanese Consulate in Kaunas, but she didn't explain the details to Masha. She just told Masha to pack because they were leaving Vilna.

Masha was bleary from sleep and wasn't sure she'd heard right when her mother told her they were going to Japan. They packed photos, mementos, clothing, and food in a bundle for the journey. They had honey cakes, which Masha's cousin had baked, and cans of sardines. They took a *drozka* — a horse-drawn "taxi" buggy — to the Vilna train station. Then they took a train to Kaunas.

Because of a medical problem, Zelda had been hemorrhaging on and off in recent weeks. She had lost a lot of blood, and was very pale and anemic. She was secretly afraid that she would die and not get Masha safely out of Europe and Russia.

They got to the official Russian travel office in Kaunas just as it was closing. The man in charge was named Mr. Goldberg. Zelda told him that they were booked to travel to Moscow by train but asked if there was a quicker way to get from Kaunas to Moscow.

Just then a Russian pilot walked into the office and announced that he had a plane that was flying to Moscow, but by regulation he couldn't fly without a full load of people; he needed two more passengers.

Zelda lamented that the refugee agency had already paid for their train trip to Moscow on the Trans-Siberian Railroad, also for their berth fees and all their food. Then Mr. Goldberg cut in, suggesting that if he exchanged Masha's food and berth coupon on the Trans-Siberian railroad, there would be enough for the flight.

So, Masha and her mother flew from Kaunas to Moscow aboard a Russian Aeroflot airplane. During the flight, Masha sat in a club chair that was uphol- stered in greenish-blue fabric. When the plane landed in Moscow, she and her mother climbed down a wooden ladder to get back on the ground.

They were told to stay in the Nova Moskovskaya Hotel in Moscow, which had once been a Czarist palace. Zelda stayed in bed because she was still hemorrhaging. Masha went up to the tenth floor where there was a restaurant and Gypsies entertaining. She asked the waitress if she could have some bread for her mother, and the waitress gave her some.

Then Masha asked for some butter, jam, and a little sugar, too. The waitress looked at her as if she were crazy and told her that nobody got butter and sugar. Did Masha think this was a capitalist country?

After a few days Zelda felt a little better. She took Masha for a walk to Red Square. Masha was wearing her coat. In Red Square they passed St. Basil's Cathedral and saw the outside of Lenin's Tomb. People came up to Masha and felt the fabric of her gray rug coat with their fingers. One man hissed the word "Capitalist!" at her.

When they packed to leave the hotel, Masha realized that her father's belt which she used with her coat had been stolen. Now she had to use a rope. Mrs. Bernstein then discovered that the four buttons that she'd been carrying with her since Warsaw had also been stolen.

They boarded the train. They had only one berth to sleep in because they'd traded the second berth and food for the plane ticket. So they shared it, sleeping head to foot like they'd slept in the room behind the piano.

When the train left Moscow, it traveled across the vast, white expanse of Russia. Masha found school friends from Warsaw and Vilna aboard the train. They played games between the cars. She noticed a group of religious students in black hats and black coats sitting bunched together. Her mother told her that they were part of the famous Mir Yeshiva.

Because she was still losing blood and was very weak, Zelda would get off at every train station and buy a bottle of blood. Then, she would drink it and lie down. Soon she'd start hemorrhaging again and lose the blood. At the next train station, she'd get off and buy another bottle of blood to drink, which was the only medical alternative at that time.

CHAPTER

29

After fourteen days on the Trans-Siberian train, they arrived in the most eastern Russian city, the port city of Vladivostok.

In Vladivostok, Zelda and Masha boarded a Japanese fishing trawler called the *Asakura Maru*. The sea was frozen thick with ice. They had to wait for an icebreaker to make a path for their ship before it could sail into the bitter cold sea.

The ship landed in the port city of Tsuruga, Japan. They were shocked to see that women worked as dockworkers and were loading and unloading cargo. At the bottom of the gangplank, they were given a box of something that looked like miniature oranges, a fruit they'd never seen before. Someone said they were called loquats.

Their group was led to the Kobe train by Japanese officials. In Kobe, they were put up in the Normandie Hotel in the European section, abutting the mountains that ringed the city. They were taken to a big room with four beds with pink satin coverlets.

After a few days they moved to a private house and shared a room with two other refugees. The house was up against a mountain, on the edge of Kobe in a section called Yamato Dori. There was a Shinto shrine on the left, and a path up the mountain on the right. When Masha walked up the path, she saw ripe raspberries growing. She picked one, ate it, picked another, filling her hands with luscious raspberries.

Zelda enrolled Masha in a French convent school, École de Ste. Marie. The students were European and Asian, the lessons were taught by French and Japanese nuns in both French and English.

There was a center for refugees in Kobe called Jewcom that was organized by the small local Jewish community and the American Jewish Joint Distribution Committee, a humanitarian agency known as the JDC. Zelda went to the center every day for their ration of a three-inch slab of white bread.

They had a Japanese transit visa to stay in Japan for twenty-five days, which had to be renewed over and over. The visa was issued for three people — Mr. and Mrs. Bernstein and Masha — but since only Masha and her mother were in Japan, and Mr. Bernstein was in prison in Vilna, there was some confusion.

After six months in Japan, their visa was cleared and they were booked on a ship called Heian Maru, which sailed from Yokohama harbor. They were put in third class. Masha somehow managed to wend her way into first class where she met several Americans. She was treated very kindly and given sweets.

Halfway through the journey, the ship stopped in mid-ocean. All the passengers were told was that cables were going back and forth between Washington and Tokyo about whether the ship could continue or would have to turn back to Japan, while tension mounted between the two countries.

Finally the ship continued on its way. It was allowed to dock in Seattle on August 1, 1941. Although they were far from Europe now, Hitler and the horrible war still seemed close by. Masha and Zelda thought of Matvey every day and about their family in Poland. Their anxiety was not lessened by the distance.

In Seattle, the American passengers got off the ship.

Masha and Zelda were transferred to a ship that was going to Vancouver in Canada. They were not allowed to set foot on American soil. The Japanese on the *Heian Maru* were sent back to Japan.

Masha saw a fat American newspaper — *The Seattle Intelligencer*. She was fascinated by American cartoons that she had first seen in Kobe — "Dick Tracy," "Little Orphan Annie," "Prince Valiant." They spent a week in Vancouver, then they were put on the Canadian Pacific Railroad train that crossed the vast breadth of Canada to Montreal.

Finally, they arrived in Montreal. It was September 1941. Although the war in Europe was even more remote now, they thought of it and read about it in the daily newspaper. Masha was enrolled in an elementary school. She told the children at school what she'd seen in Warsaw, and about their escape to Lithuania and then across Russia to Japan.

Within the past two years Masha had gone from speaking Yiddish and Polish to learning some Lithuanian, Russian, and Japanese, and now was learning English and French. Several parents of schoolmates went to see Masha and told her that she was making up terrible stories about life in Warsaw and was giving their children nightmares.

The children in the school knitted scarves and washcloths for Canadian and British soldiers overseas. Masha spoke about her father all the time. She told whoever would listen that her father was in prison and that she didn't know whether he was dead or alive.

But Sugihara visa No. 1882 had brought Masha and her mother this far.

30

The Sugiharas left Prague by car in March. Powdery snow fell, piling up on the windshield of the car. After they crossed the border into Germany, the road got icy and the car slipped and slid. Soon the road became mountainous. As they reached the top of the mountain range, the sun was setting behind the mountains.

Suddenly, the car skidded on ice. Yukiko grabbed for her children as the car spun off the road and began to slide across the ice as though it were going to fly into the valley. But — just before disaster — the car came to a stop.

Königsberg was a quiet German town between Lithuania and Poland. The lowland countryside had fertile soil and extensive forests where the Dukes of Prussia had once been crowned. The family lived in a large house that was two stories high and had a garden for Mr. Sugihara to cultivate. It also had a little orchard attached that had pear and apple trees. The Japanese consulate began to function immediately.

Chiune and Yukiko did some entertaining, mainly inviting members of the diplomatic community to small dinners. Although people had been put on ration coupons and were not eating very well, this didn't include diplomats, who could still get good food, real coffee, and other things that were hard to come by.

With the arrival of spring, the fruit trees blossomed. Then, with pink and white blossoms blowing in the wind and filling the air with sweet smells, Sugihara planted his vegetables. He organized his watering cans and tools. Many little squirrels ran up and down the branches of the trees.

Yukiko gave Hiroki a bag of peanuts and told him to feed the squirrels. When she looked out of the window, she saw bushy squirrels climbing onto Hiroki's shoulder and eating out of his hand and out of the hands of his little brothers.

When the weather became too warm, Yukiko opened the windows of the house to let in fresh air. As soon as she did, the friendly squirrels climbed inside.

In high school, Chiune Sugihara, shown here at age seventeen, realized that he wanted to be a teacher, not a doctor as his father wished. (Sugihara Family; Eric Saul, Curator)

Sugihara studied at China's Harbin School, but had to leave for a year of military training and service; in this 1920 photograph, he wears his military uniform. (Sugihara Family; Eric Saul, Curator)

In 1935, Sugihara met and married Yukiko Kikuchi. (Sugihara Family; Eric Saul, Curator)

Sugihara and his family arrived in Kaunas (also known as Kovno), Lithuania, in 1939. There, he was Japan's vice consul to Lithuania. (Permission of YIVO/USHMM)

A forced labor brigade in the Kovno Ghetto. (Courtesy of Simon Wiesenthal Center Library and Archives, Los Angeles, California, and in memory of George Kadish)

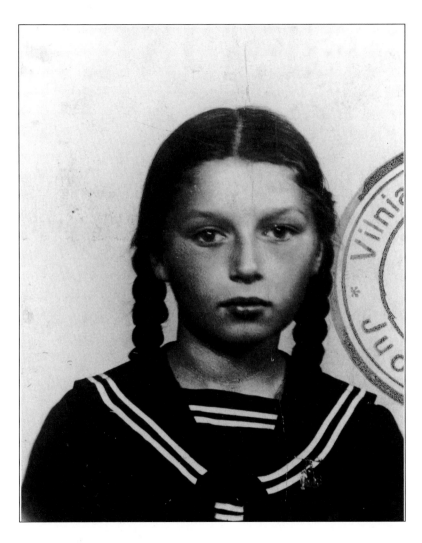

After Adolf Hitler's army attacked Warsaw, Poland, Masha Bernstein's family escaped to Lithuania. She is nine years old in this photograph from 1940. (Masha Leon)

Masha and her parents, Zelda and Matvey, in Vilna, Lithuania. (Masha Leon)

A group of Polish-Jewish refugees celebrate at a Passover Seder in Lithuania. (Sugihara Family; Eric Saul, Curator)

Desperate for exit visas, refugees crowded outside the gate of Sugihara's Japanese Consulate in Kovno. (Setsuko Kikuchi/Sugihara Family; Eric Saul, Curator)

Solly Ganor, shown here in 1945, was only eleven years old when he met Chiune Sugihara and invited him to his family's Chanukah party. (Permission of Solly Ganor)

Sugihara often drove out in the humid countryside to do his work for the Japanese government. As he drove, he listened to the yellow birds calling to each other with three sad notes. Sugihara was gathering information on new troop movements on both sides of the Russian-German border and realized that the war might reach them at any moment.

While he was away on an intelligence-gathering trip, Yukiko took the children swimming in the chilly Baltic Sea. They gaped at what they saw on a beach close by — nudists sunning and swimming.

CHAPTER

31

Solly Ganor woke early to feed bread crumbs to a friendly pigeon that belonged to his neighbor. The pigeon's name was Queenie. The sun was just coming up over Kaunas, a pink smudge of dawn. Mist rose from the roofs. Solly looked out over the rooftops and noticed gray puffs of smoke in the sky and then he heard the sound of guns.

The Ganor family huddled around the radio. It announced that Hitler had broken the Nonaggression Pact and was attacking Russia. The Nazi army was also on their way to invade Lithuania. Chaim and Rebecca Ganor deeply regretted that they hadn't tried to use Sugihara's visas to leave the country when they still could. How foolish they had been to wait to sell the business. They'd now waited too long and the visas were useless.

Solly's family decided to try to escape toward the Russian border. They packed a few things and went to the railroad station, but were turned away. So they walked toward the road that led out of the city. German Stuka airplanes flew over and strafed fleeing people and the road with bullets.

Along the road, the Ganors witnessed gangs of armed Lithuanians, sometimes called *Siauliai*, rounding up and shooting unarmed Jewish people. Among them Solly saw his history teacher, her husband, and five-year-old daughter shot. In the distance Solly also saw yellow flashes and blue smoke. He heard rifle shots behind a massive stone wall that circled an old fort on the outskirts of Kaunas.

After sleeping in barns and hiding in the woods, Solly's family realized that escape was hopeless. They made their way back to Kaunas, to their apartment on Kalviu Street. All except Herman, who had mysteriously vanished along the way.

Very quickly, food became scarce for everyone, but especially hard for Jews to acquire since *Siauliai* would injure or kill Jews if they saw them on a food line or out in the street. Because it was less dangerous for young people to go outside, Solly and his sister, Fanny, often scavenged for food for the entire family.

One day Fanny went off ahead. As Solly caught up with her, he saw her being pulled like a dog into a side street by a gang of Siauliai. They'd put a rope around her neck. Her nose was bleeding. Her dress was ripped.

Without thinking, Solly rammed himself into the Lithuanian who was pulling the rope. The rowdy man was so drunk that when the rope jumped out of his hand Solly was able to grab Fanny's hand, pull sharply, and the two of them ran so fast they got away.

After that, Fanny fell into a depression and wouldn't go outside. So Solly had to go out by himself to search for bread and scraps of food for the family.

On June 25, in the dead of night, Lithuanians stormed the Jewish neighborhood and slaughtered approximately 700 Jewish people. In the morning, when Solly went outside to find food he saw blood-spattered walls. He also saw limbs of human beings that had been hacked off bodies and thrown into the street. The man in front of him on the food line, who obviously didn't realize that Solly was Jewish, laughed and described how the drunkest Siauliai played soccer with Jewish heads.

By July 10 the Germans had clearly taken charge. A proclamation was nailed to every building which stated: *All persons of Jewish origin are ordered to move to Slabodke no later than August 15, 1941.*

On August 7, the Ganor family filled a borrowed wagon with some of their possessions and crossed the Vilijampole Bridge into the new Jewish ghetto called Slabodke. They were lucky that they left that morning because, in the afternoon, over a thousand Jewish men were arrested. These men were taken to a secret spot and one by one, they were shot.

The Ganors' ghetto apartment consisted of a bedroom and living room. There was no kitchen, no bathroom, no running water, just a wood stove. They and the other Jews in the ghetto were organized into labor brigades by the Germans. These brigades were sent out of the ghetto each morning to work and returned at night.

Everybody in the ghetto was put on rations. The per-week ration for one person was: less than a kilo of bread; 125 grams of horse meat; 122 grams of flour; 75 grams of coffee substitute; 50 grams of salt; and a few potatoes.

The daily struggle for food became the center of all their thoughts. All day and night the gate to the ghetto was locked shut. It was guarded by German soldiers and Lithuanian policemen. Very quickly Solly's aunts and uncles and cousins moved into the two small rooms with Solly's family because they had nowhere else to go. All the apartments in the ghetto were full.

They hoped that somehow Herman would find them if he was still alive.

32

Although war raged all across Europe in 1941, as winter approached, it hadn't reached Königsberg. In Königsberg, Chiune and Yukiko eventually got used to Hitler youth and local people greeting them with the Nazi salute and "Heil Hitler."

Sugihara sent secret reports to the Japanese government. He reported that trains filled with German soldiers were massing in Königsberg. He reported seeing ten steamships moored in ice-free Pilau Port, which was linked with the Baltic by a canal. He reported that the German army was concentrating troops in East Prussia. He reported that German officers were being taught rudimentary Russian and map-reading.

To take their minds off the war, Yukiko organized a special Japanese event for Hiroki, Chiaki, Haruki, and the other children in the neighborhood. On a day with blue skies and only a few fat clouds, all were invited to fly special *koinobori*, which are brightly colored Japanese kites shaped like carp. There was just enough wind that day, the children flew the carp kites high. In Japan, these kites symbolize strength and courage.

Every day Chiune and Yukiko listened attentively to the radio. When news was broadcast that Germans had attacked Lithuania and had occupied the country, they looked at each other and wondered what had happened to their refugees; how many, if any, had made it out of Lithuania?

All they'd been able to do since leaving Kaunas was to pray that their refugees had arrived safely at their destinations. They thought often — with *giri* and *on*, the Japanese virtues of responsibility for others — about those people who they remembered so vividly.

They also worried and thought about their friends in Kaunas — Solly and Chaim Ganor, and their large family — and wondered if they'd used the visas Chiune had given them or if they'd been trapped in Kaunas when the Nazis arrived. They prayed that they would survive whatever was to come.

There was so little anyone could do to relieve suffering, but sometimes Yukiko was able to give a little extra coffee to the mothers of her children's friends.

In November 1941 after work, Chiune sat with Yukiko. He told her that the Foreign Ministry had written a letter to him suggesting that he should send his family back to Japan. Yukiko looked distraught. She wanted to stay with Chiune, she wanted her husband and sons to be together. Even if they all died.

In Königsberg they witnessed anti-Jewish edicts: All Jews were ordered to wear yellow stars. Jews could no longer shop in regular stores, go to restaurants, or sit in the parks. Jewish bank accounts were frozen. Jewish jobs were terminated.

In December, British bombers continued to fly into German airspace and drop bombs on Germany. Then, on December 7, 1941, Japan attacked the United States at Pearl Harbor in Hawaii. The following day the United States entered the war.

CHAPTER

33

As part of their official duty, Consul and Mrs. Sugihara were invited to attend a ceremony at the grave of General von Hindenburg, the former president of Germany. Along with high-ranking officers, other diplomats, and Hindenburg's grandson, they stood beside Hindenburg's grave. Those attending were asked to pray for victory but Chiune and Yukiko had no doubt that — as of the fall and winter of 1941 — the tide of the war was turning against Hitler.

When Japan joined the war, the Sugiharas' houseboy noticed a map of Japan in the morning newspaper. After breakfast, when he brought Mr. Sugihara the newspaper and the day's mail, he joked about how small Japan really was. Wouldn't someone in Japan fall into the sea if they tripped?

Chiune smiled. He realized that it was true. To Europeans, Japan was a faraway string of tiny islands in a remote part of the world. Sugihara had been against Japan's participation in the war and had predicted to his wife that the war would be a mistake for Japan.

When the houseboy had gone, Mr. Sugihara put the newspaper aside and opened his letters. In one envelope was an order to shut the consulate in Königsberg. He was officially informed that his next posting would be in Bucharest, Romania. But first, Sugihara was again ordered to Berlin to report to his superior.

So Yukiko packed everything, and the entire family went to Berlin.

Just as they were arriving at the hotel in Berlin, in the early fall of 1942, an air raid siren shrieked. Yukiko, Chiune, and Setsuko grabbed the children's hands and ran to the elevator that took them to the shelter. Their hearts thumped with fear until the all-clear sounded.

They went back up to their rooms. But no sooner were the children tucked into their beds, than the siren wailed again. Back into the elevator they went. Inside the elevator stood a pale, blond German woman. As the elevator dropped down to the shelter, the woman muttered to no one and everyone that Germany would never be defeated, would fight until the end, would recover any lost ground!

Sugihara politely ignored the mutterings of this woman. She could declaim all she liked, but Sugihara knew that Germany *would* be defeated. It was simply a matter of how long it would take and how much more blood would have to be lost.

It was late fall, a time of cold rain and frozen puddles, by the time they got to Bucharest, Romania. Bucharest was already occupied by German soldiers. Swatstika flags flew from poles everywhere, portraits of Hitler were on walls in every office and house. Sugihara was given a grand mansion on an elegant street. He was glad to discover that delicious *mititei* — pork sausages — could still be purchased by diplomats in Bucharest.

The war got worse everywhere, including Romania. Because of the war, Ambassador Ashima, the man who Sugihara was replacing, was unable to book passage to Japan, so he stayed at his post. This meant that Sugihara couldn't officially assume his position. Instead, he did translations for the legation, the diplomatic ministry staff and office.

Though the war was raging everywhere around them, their life was undramatic. Yukiko studied the seven-string classical Russian guitar. She arranged for the children to study violin and accordion. Music filled their house.

Hiroki, now eight years old, brought a little girl home one day and told his parents that she was his girlfriend. Chiune and Yukiko hid their humor and shock. Yes, their children were growing up.

Their house was so well located on the most important street in Bucharest that the children could watch special parades from their window. They saw King Mikhail, the Romanian king, lead a parade. Also, they saw performing dogs and dancing bears, which were favorite forms of entertainment in Romania.

Finally bombs began to fall on Bucharest.

To get his family away from the bombing, Chiune found a house for them beside a lovely lake in the area filled with legends about Count Dracula. The legend said that this was his burial place. Although they were several miles away from the city, they could still hear the explosions that sounded like approaching thunder. They could still see dark, menacing smoke curling toward the heavens in the distance.

In Stalingrad, Russians were fighting for their lives. In North Africa, the Germans were experiencing their first defeats.

34

By the winter of 1943 the tide had turned against Hitler. Germany had been defeated in Stalingrad, and the Allies had begun to advance into Italy, pushing the Nazis back. Japan had quickly lost much of its Pacific fleet and was in danger of losing the war.

Outside Bucharest, Chiune and Yukiko skied between pine trees while the children made snowmen. In the distance they could hear the muted sound of bombs.

When summer came, Sugihara found a little white cottage about an hour's drive from Bucharest. He moved his family into the cottage, which was bordered by a row of tall poplars. Now they were farther away from the bombing targets. Safe, he hoped. Sugihara worked in his rose garden. He took the children for boat rides on a nearby lake, which was dazzling in the sunshine.

On Sundays, with a bag of *covrigis* — chewy pretzels — for the children, the family piled into the car and drove into the countryside. Often their car was the only automobile, threading in and out to avoid hitting farmers in wagons who were taking their families to church. Once, what looked like a fluffy white cloud rolled down a hill toward them. Chiune stopped the car. A large mass of white sheep moved toward the car taking up the entire road.

In spite of Sugihara's schemes to protect the family from the falling bombs, the bombing got closer and he had a bomb shelter built beside their cottage. Still the bombing grew worse. More of Bucharest and its environs were being destroyed every day.

In another attempt to protect his family, Sugihara moved even farther away, to a little town called Poiana Brasov, where he rented a house.

While driving through Bucharest on their way to Poiana Brasov, they saw how much destruction had befallen Bucharest. The children couldn't believe it when they saw a car sitting on the roof of a building. The car must have been blown there by the blast of a large bomb.

The sirens roared. This meant that another attack was coming. Chiune tried to get them speedily out of town, but the attack started by the time they'd gotten to the country road, which was filled with black, acrid smoke. Sugihara couldn't see to drive and the children became frightened.

When they got to Poiana Brasov, parts of the town had also been bombed. Sugihara drove rapidly up the hill to their new little house in the forest. Mercifully, their house was untouched. Above the house, curious crows circled the sky.

Daily the air raids grew worse. Regardless of the danger, it was necessary for Sugihara to go into Bucharest on consulate business. One time when he was away, there was a very large air raid. Setsuko and Yukiko decided to drive to Brasov to see how much damage had been done. The chauffeur reluctantly took them. The chauffeur knew that Chiune would not like it, but couldn't refuse Mrs. Sugihara's request.

Yukiko and Setsuko saw terrible damage in the town. They saw dead bodies being piled into the back of a truck. Setsuko noticed something strange on the road. She got out to look. Yukiko heard her scream. She jumped back into the car. She was deathly pale. She had seen a severed human leg.

35

In *the Kaunas ghetto*, the problem of hunger escalated quickly. Solly, his father, and uncles were put into work gangs. Every night they returned to the ghetto, hungry, blistered, and exhausted. Solly worked with the weeding brigade.

During the first week that they were in the ghetto, 500 Jewish men were rounded up and taken away. They were never heard from again. Rumor had it that the men had been taken to a fort near Panemune and shot.

During the second week, after his father and uncles had already gone to work, and while his mother was out, Solly was awakened by four German policemen.

They were looking for valuables. One growled and squeezed his neck tightly, demanding that Solly tell him where they were hiding their gold and jewelry.

His Aunt Dobbe and Cousin Miriam quickly gave over a wedding ring and some family silver to the policemen.

A few days later, Solly saw orphans removed from the orphanage and put into trucks. He saw elderly people carried from the old age home. He saw sick people removed from the hospital. All were driven in trucks or forced to walk on foot up the hill to the Ninth Fort while the German officer in charge stood coldly with his hands on his hips.

Solly saw Aunt Leena rush toward Uncle Jacob to shield him when a German soldier unholstered his pistol. But before she could get close, the soldier shot Uncle Jacob in the back. Then, he shot Jacob in the head. Solly heard Aunt Leena scream. He saw Uncle Jacob's knees buckle, then saw him fall forward.

The next day, looking up from his work, Solly glimpsed long columns of Jews marching to the road that led to the Ninth Fort. As he watched, a flock of birds suddenly rose up from a field and, beating their wings, flew south. Solly longed to be a bird.

All day and night the sound of gunfire was heard from the Ninth Fort. Some people mourned and some gratefully said the *Gomel*, the Jewish blessing said by those who have been given a reprieve from sudden death.

About two thousand people went to their deaths that day.

The following month, Solly had the good fortune to make contact with a Lithuanian who offered to smuggle food into the ghetto. On the appointed night, Solly waited at the ghetto fence. He waited for a low whistle, which was the signal. When it came, he saw his contact in the shadows across the street. He saw the contact swing a bag twice around his head and watched the bag fly over the fence. Just as Solly grabbed the bag, the spotlight went on.

The guard was looking down at him through the sight of a raised rifle. He shouted at Solly, wanting to know if there were any cigarettes in the bag. Then he declared that if there were cigarettes, Solly would win his life; if there weren't, he'd be dead.

Solly closed his eyes and braced for death. He heard the click of the safety catch. He emptied the bag. Out rolled bread, carrots, but no cigarettes. The guard said that it looked like he'd won his life, and called him "boy." Then the soldier told him to hand over the cig-arettes and get away.

Solly was astounded, confused. Both of them could

see that there were no cigarettes in the bag. The guard laughed. He reached into his pocket, held up his own cigarettes, and quipped that the cigarettes were in his hand, now Solly should get away before he changed his mind.

Solly grabbed the bread and carrots and ran. Every muscle in his body was quivering. He realized that he'd just experienced a miracle. He realized that he'd just encountered a decent human being!

He ran until he got to his apartment.

CHAPTER 36

On a frosty morning in October 1941, the Germans made the entire ghetto population of Kaunas — about 25,000 men, women, and children — assemble in Demokratu Square and stand in columns. The Kommandant of the ghetto — Herr Jordan — and the Gestapo boss of Jewish affairs — Herr Rauca — went through every column. They selected those who would go to the left, and those who would go to the right. Solly felt like he was drowning in fright as he waited. When his turn came, he, his mother, father, and Fanny were sent to the left.

Separated families screamed. The ones sent to the right were marched out of the square. Then Solly and the others were allowed to go back to their apartments.

At home, Mrs. Ganor made cups of *kaffee ersatz*. The family sat together. They were overwhelmed.

Suddenly, the door flew open. Aunt Anushka and Uncle Jochil and their children stood in the doorway. The reunited families fell on one another with happiness. But then Fanny screamed. Her knees buckled. The others joined her at the window and saw what had affected her. In the distance, through the gray light, they could see a column of people snaking slowly up the hill toward the Ninth Fort. It seemed like there were miles of people, that the line was endless.

The winding road that went up to the Ninth Fort was visible from everywhere in the ghetto. For two more days, an unending line of Jews could be seen climbing, and the sound of machine-gun fire could be heard echoing through the streets. In every house the Jewish prayer for the dead — *Kaddish* — was said, and said again. And again. Nine thousand people of the Kaunas ghetto were murdered in this "big action," as the Germans called it.

Then, captured Jews who had been sent by the Nazis from other parts of Europe began arriving at the Kaunas train station. They were quickly sent to the Ninth Fort and murdered.

The winter was so cold. When Solly and Fanny and Chaim and Uncle Jochil returned from work, the others had to massage their frozen hands for hours to bring back the circulation. But their luck held and they remained alive. People they knew got frostbite, some so badly that they'd lose a limb, but none of Solly's family did. That New Year's Eve, church bells rang through the freezing, dark night. Accompanying the ringing bells was the unending sound of machine-gun fire.

By spring of 1944, only about five thousand of the original 25,000 Kaunas ghetto dwellers remained alive. Solly had turned sixteen.

In July, word spread that the entire ghetto was being evacuated to a concentration camp near Danzig. Solly heard that they would not be sent by train, but would be put on barges and floated down the Niemunas River. This was very frightening because the rumor was that the Germans put people on boats and drowned them.

But when the time came, Solly and his parents were lined up with those who remained in the ghetto. They were marched though the Varniu Gate, then across the Vilijampole Bridge. Solly looked back at the ghetto and saw fire and smoke pouring from the buildings. He heard explosions because the Germans were gutting the ghetto.

Rather than being put onto a barge, they marched for two hours. Then the Ganor family was packed into a cattle car so tightly that no one could possibly lie down to sleep. It was stifling, with only two small openings covered with barbed wire to let in any ventilation.

The door of the cattle car was shut, and the train began to move off, away from Kaunas, away from Lithuania, away from Solly's childhood home and possibly, away from Herman. It gathered speed.

CHAPTER

37

In March 1944, *Russia accelerated* its attack on Romania. Sugihara told Yukiko that they'd have to leave soon.

In May, Yukiko went alone — with car and driver — into Bucharest to rescue some personal items she'd forgotten there. She left a message for her husband that she'd be back before nightfall.

Part of the way to Bucharest, the car broke down. The driver said he would fix it, so Yukiko accepted a ride in a German military car. Just before the military car entered Bucharest, it was stopped by a German soldier who warned them that the German army had been defeated in Bucharest. They should stay away from the city because it was very dangerous. The soldier suggested they'd be better off going into the forest.

Joining the retreating soldiers, the car Yukiko was in drove into the forest with other cars. Yukiko could hear the sounds of gunfire and shells bursting. A soldier told the driver that the road was closed.

Yukiko was left alone in the car. She felt very nervous so she got out and walked toward a stand of pine trees. In her mind she imagined Chiune and her beautiful children. Their faces were vivid.

A young, handsome officer in a blue uniform wearing a German medal approached Yukiko. He told her that his name was Dürer and that it was impossible for her to get out of the forest alone. He suggested that it would be safer if Yukiko left with him. He and others were trying to cross the border into Germany.

When night fell, Dürer put her in his car. Another soldier brought her bread, greasy soup, and stew in a metal bowl, then a little later he brought her a blanket. The soup was awful. Yukiko curled up on the car seat and fell asleep. A moon rose in the sky, then slid behind the trees.

Yukiko was in the forest with the retreating army for eight days. During this time, Dürer spoke with Yukiko about himself, and listened while she told him about her family, about Japan. All around them, German soldiers leaned and sat against trees. The mood was grim, since all chances of victory had faded away. Late at night, an eerie windstorm blew through the forest. Yukiko listened to the howling dirge of the wind as the hours slowly passed.

Before that night was over, Dürer opened the car door and told Yukiko that the time they'd both feared had arrived. He put Yukiko next to him in the front of the car and began to drive. She thanked Dürer for protecting her.

When the car stopped bouncing, Yukiko realized that Dürer had driven onto the paved road. A bombardment was in progress. As he drove, the bombs dropped close to them. Strangely, she felt no fear, even when flames and flashes burst in front of their car and a truck full of soldiers just ahead of them exploded. Yukiko saw dead and dying soldiers on the side of the road.

All around were flames. The sky itself was tinged with red.

Suddenly, shells exploded all around them. Dürer shouted for her to get out of the car. She did. She felt him push her down into bushy grass, and throw himself on top of her to protect her with his body. Yukiko began to cry. With one eye, she could see a soldier running toward her, aiming his rifle at her head. In the light of a shellburst, the enemy caught her eye. She saw a strange look of shock on his face at seeing a Japanese lady in the Romanian brush.

She heard the gun cock, but went into shock and heard nothing else. All noise disappeared. In her mind, she saw her family in a room so bright it was blinding.

When Yukiko came to, she was lying alone in the grass. Pale light of dawn was coming through the trees. The battle had ended. She saw Dürer's body lying a short distance away as if he were asleep. She called out his name.

He didn't answer. She touched him. He was dead.

Dürer and the other dead were buried in makeshift graves. Yukiko knelt at his grave.

The surviving German soldiers began to walk toward the German border, helping the wounded and bleeding. Yukiko walked the other way, back into Romania, toward Brasov. It was hard to walk because her right heel was torn away, but she was determined to find Chiune and her children.

She thought about Dürer, buried without a headstone. She felt the weight of sadness for Dürer and thought of the misery of so many wounded on both sides, and also of the desperate faces of the thousands of refugees outside her window in Kaunas. She felt terrible, terrible sadness for all of them.

Finally she saw a farmhouse. She went to the door and told the farmer that she was the wife of a diplomat and she needed help.

CHAPTER

38

Yukiko *had been gone* for eight days. Mr. Sugihara had looked frantically for her, had risked his life by going behind lines into the battle to search. By the fifth day he held little hope that she was alive. When he saw her emerge from the car of a stranger, he sprang up to greet her.

The children and Setsuko ran outside, too, and looked up at Yukiko's dirty face. They waited for her to explain what had happened. Instead of speaking, she began to laugh. Her laughter rose and fell like a roller coaster even though tears were seeping from her eyes. She walked into her house surrounded by Chiune, her sister, and her grateful children.

Finally after years of losing protracted battles, the German army surrendered to the Allies on May 8, 1945. The victorious Soviets escorted Sugihara and his family to the Japanese legation in Bucharest along with other diplomats. They were guarded by soldiers. The children were not allowed to play outside. A kind Russian soldier gave the children a turtle. The children made a little house for the turtle with stones.

In August 1945 the Japanese surrendered, too.

Sugihara didn't know what would be done to them. Yukiko packed their things, gave her kimonos away to the neighbor to whom she'd spoken across the fence. This neighbor lady whispered that the situation was very bad now. It would be very bad for her children if they sent her to Siberia. She offered to take the responsibility for bringing up all three children.

The woman persisted, urging Yukiko to lift the children over the fence to her. Yukiko thanked her for her kindness, but told her that she couldn't bear the thought of losing her children.

Three days later, a Soviet officer came into the Japanese legation. As Yukiko and the children stood paralyzed with fear, he took Mr. Sugihara into the conference room.

The waiting was interminable, but finally Chiune came out of the room. He was unharmed. No one could read his feelings on his face. He told Yukiko to pack their bags, that they were being sent to an internment camp.

It started to rain as they packed their things, which were quickly put into a truck. The rain turned the dust to mud. The woman next door and her children waved and watched as the truck drove away.

39

Solly, *Fanny, Chaim, Rebecca, and Aunt Anushka* were taken off the train at Stutthof, Germany. They were at a concentration camp encircled by electric fencing, barbed wire, and watchtowers with machine guns. They were put into tattered, striped prison uniforms and caps and were left in a kind of storage room that held piles of shoes. They stayed there until morning.

When he awoke in the morning, Solly saw his mother standing over him. She whispered that they were going to be separated today, she didn't know when they'd see each other again.

Shortly, the door opened, and an SS officer ordered everyone to get out quickly. He called them "Jewish swine." He told the women and children to go one way and the men to go another. He told them to leave everything behind.

As the women were marched away, Rebecca Ganor looked back. Her eyes met and held Solly's. She smiled deeply into his eyes, piercing his heart. She held her head high. Solly watched her until she was out of sight.

When the women and children had gone, Solly and his father were lined up military fashion in a big square. They were taught to take their caps off, to smack them smartly against their legs in unison when the Capo shouted "Mützen ab! Caps off!"

They were assigned a barracks and given jobs. Chaim Ganor's job was to divide rations because he was able to cut bread into perfectly even slices.

After many months of this terrible life, Solly and his father were transported out of the camp. They were taken by train through Germany. From the train, they could see hundreds of bombs falling on a city in the distance. They heard terrible explosions and sirens and saw searchlights crisscrossing the night sky.

In the towns of Landsberg and Kaufering, Germany, they were marched to a camp that was a new slave-labor addition to Dachau concentration camp. Again, as weak as they'd become, Solly and Chaim tried to impress the SS by whipping off their caps, slapping them smartly against their legs. Here food rations were so skimpy that Solly almost fainted when he was loading a cart at his work detail and smelled food cooking.

In the summer of 1944, the camp buzzed with news of the Allied landing at Normandy. Hope was briefly rekindled despite hunger and disease. But, by October, starvation, hard labor, lice, and disease had taken many more lives. Few prisoners survived more than a few weeks in these camps.

During the night, Solly watched bombardments above him as American and British planes flew into Germany. The months passed grimly.

On Christmas morning, Solly and his father were astonished to each receive a winter coat with a large white X painted across the back. They were old coats, but they were warm. Christmas day was Chaim's birthday. On Christmas afternoon there was no work to do. Chaim fell asleep. He abruptly bolted awake and shouted at Solly that his mother was dead.

Chaim wept. Solly tried to calm him by telling him he'd been having a nightmare, but he was inconsolable. Chaim claimed that he'd actually seen his wife, and cried, "My life's companion" and "My sweet Rebecca!"

In April, they'd been on starvation rations for more

than a month when they were told that they were being force-marched to the main camp at Dachau. Chaim, Solly, and Solly's new friend, a young man named Bertholt, marched together.

When they reached Dachau they were joined by other Jews and also non-Jewish Russians, Poles, Belgians, French, and other political prisoners of the Germans, and told that the march would continue.

Again they marched together — Bertholt, another new friend named Jacob, Chaim, and Solly. They marched day after day. Often the guards beat and cursed them. German shepherds and vicious Doberman dogs lunged at them. Most of the prisoners on this "death march" were killed in the nearly two weeks that it lasted.

In the second week, it began to rain and the temperature dropped. They passed a place called Wolfratshausen and were marched into the woods. They heard gunfire in the distance. "It's the Americans!" Solly shouted, and threw his hat into the air.

The prisoners hugged and slapped one another on the back. Then, with a funny, drunken smile on his face, Jacob slid to the ground.

Chaim held Jacob in his arms, begging him not to die, not to leave him, and called him Herman. Chaim clutched the dead boy and rocked him, calling "Herman, Herman."

Solly remembered Sugihara's last words to him and whispered them to Jacob, *Vaya con Dios.*

His father wept, then refused to speak. Both he and Solly were on the verge of death from exhaustion and hunger.

The following day, the chilly rain turned to snow. Spring daffodils and tulips were coated. They stopped near a town called Waachirchen. There, that night, in a final act of cruelty, the German and Ukrainian guards attempted to murder the few remaining Jewish survivors. Many of the prisoners hid in the snow and avoided being shot.

It was May. Solly and the others fell exhausted into the snow in the woods and slept.

In the first light, Solly woke. Around him were a few huddling Jewish prisoners coated with snow. It was entirely silent. He felt nothing anymore. In the distance he saw a tank. It had a white star on is side. Then he saw a jeep.

Soldiers got out of the jeep and walked toward him. He closed his eyes and waited to be hit with a bullet, but instead he heard words in English.

He opened his eyes. Above him stood a soldier with

kind eyes and Asian features, a man that reminded Solly of Mr. Sugihara. The man said, "You are free, boy. You're free now."

Solly asked the soldier's name.

He replied that he was a Japanese-American with the U.S. Army. His name was Clarence Matsamura from Wyoming.

Clarence gave Solly a chocolate bar with the word Hershey's on it. It was one of the few acts of kindness shown to him by a soldier in more than five years. And then Clarence asked Solly his name. Solly told him he was Solly Ganor, a Jewish boy from Kaunas, Lithuania.

40

When the war ended, Masha and Zelda Bernstein were still in Montreal, Canada. They had received one post-card from Matvey Bernstein in 1943, but nothing else. They didn't know if he was dead or alive, but every day Masha and Zelda wrote a letter to him, never knowing if he received any of them.

They learned that Poland had become a graveyard, that every one of Masha's forty-five cousins had been killed by the Nazis. All her aunts, uncles, and both sets of grandparents had also been murdered. They had no one now and did what they could to get information about Matvey, hoping against hope that he was alive.

About a week after Victory in Europe Day — May 8, 1945 — they received a letter from the Canadian government informing them that Canada was happy to have hosted them through the war, but now the war was over. They were being repatriated to Poland. Or, "to the graveyard" as Zelda called it.

Zelda tried to think of every possible way to get to America and not be sent back to Europe. Unfortunately, their old papers, including the visa given in Kaunas, were no longer valid. Grasping at straws, Zelda suggested to Masha that she write a letter to Mrs. Roosevelt.

So Masha wrote an eleven-page letter to Eleanor Roosevelt, the widow of President Franklin Roosevelt, who was known to be a kind and compassionate lady. Masha wrote the letter in pencil.

A reply was delivered from the American Consulate in Montreal. The letter said: *Please come to see the American consul.*

When they walked into the consul's office the official was holding a dossier. He looked at Masha and, with a big smile on his face, asked Masha if she was the little girl who had written to Mrs. Roosevelt.

Masha said that she was the one.

He told them that their past papers were now invalid. But he'd help them get new documents to go to America.

His friendly smile made both Masha and Zelda's hearts leap with hope that they might not have to go back to the graveyard of Poland. Zelda told him that they had cousins in Chicago and the consul thought that would certainly help.

In August 1945, they arrived in Chicago where their American relatives were willing to sponsor them. Shortly after they arrived, they learned that Matvey Bernstein had survived. He'd spent time in Siberia, and time in Tashkent, the capital of Uzbekistan. He'd spent a year in solitary confinement where he maintained his sanity by writing down the names of over 100,000 people he had met in the course of his life. He'd been released from prison and had gone back to Poland. However, he could not come to the United States because the quotas for Polish immigrants were full.

Matvey Bernstein went to Argentina instead. When Masha was older, Zelda Bernstein went down and joined her husband there.

Masha, however, did not see her father for nineteen years.

CHAPTER
41

At first the Sugiharas were put into two rooms of an old army barracks near Bucharest. Most of their personal possessions were confiscated by the Russian soldiers, including Yukiko's precious family photographs. Yukiko later convinced an officer to return the photographs as they were personal mementos of her family.

The only warmth was from a drafty coal stove. They slept on straw mattresses. They were confined indoors except for once a day, when they could take a walk in the barracks square and take a breath of fresh air. Their only food was a foul soup prepared by German prisoners. Occasionally, they could buy a few vegetables from an old farmer who was allowed to sell his wares.

The seasons changed. Rain crashed on the roof and trees bent from heavy snow on the branches. Their routine remained unchanged. One day near Christmas, their former neighbor was brought to see them. The guards had allowed her through. Her eyelashes were white and frozen, there was snow on her hat and the shoulders of her coat. She explained that she felt sorry for the children having to face a Christmas with no gifts and handed Yukiko a cake that she had baked.

Except for small concerts given by several German prisoners — violin, piano, and singing — life was monotonous and grim.

The year 1946 arrived. The stupefying routine remained unchanged. Another year passed, and their second Christmas in internment was approaching.

One December morning the air smelled like snow and it began to snow. First thing in the morning, Chiune was visited by a Soviet officer. He told Sugihara he was allowing him and his family to return to Japan and that they would be leaving immediately.

Chiune told Yukiko to please pack their things.

Yukiko packed and bundled the children in several layers of clothes. There was nothing Yukiko could do about the lice and fleas that infested their clothing and their bodies. The children and she and Chiune wore their fur coats because they were going into the Soviet winter.

The children asked where they were going. Yukiko told them that they were going back to Japan and the children smiled happily, although they remembered nothing of Japan and only Hiroki had been there.

They were put into a truck. The snow was very deep and fat flakes were falling thicker and thicker when the driver turned on the engine. It was hard for the truck to drive in deep snow, and its wheels spun. Then the tires found traction and gripped the road. Chiune and Yukiko looked back at the barracks where they'd spent so many hundreds of monotonous days, but quickly the driving snow obscured the sight.

They were put into a freight train with hard benches. The only heat came from a small wood-burning stove. They lived and slept in their fur hats, fur boots, and fur coats. They were tormented by lice and fleas. When the train stopped, they could hear a loud banging noise that meant that a Soviet soldier was breaking off pieces of urine that had frozen to the side of the train where the slop bucket had been tossed.

For more than a month the train crawled across Russia, past birch forests, past golden domed churches. Outside was an endless expanse of snowy Russia, the same route that many of Sugihara's Jewish visa holders from Kaunas would have taken. Fires were lit at crossroads.

Very often the children would ask if they would ever truly be allowed to return to Japan. Mr. Sugihara stood with his back straight and watched a forest of white birches. He was wondering the same thing.

Finally the train stopped and they were loaded into a truck that drove them through weather reaching 45 degrees below zero to another internment camp. They were in Odessa and could actually see the rough, inky waves of the Black Sea through wet snowflakes.

For three more months they were shuttled from internment camp to internment camp. Finally they were herded into a room with seventeen other prisoners in an internment camp surrounded by barbed wire. They were in a port called Nakhodka, which looked out on the Sea of Japan. Again the food was bread and greasy soup. Again there was almost no heat and they had to sleep in their filthy, stinking fur coats.

On the other side of the barbed wire were Japanese prisoners whose job was to chop down trees and saw lumber. The icy snow crackled under their feet as they worked. These were the first Japanese the family had seen in many years. One day, one of the prisoners borrowed Hiroki's violin and played lovely music for all the prisoners. Mr. Sugihara listened and pined for home.

CHAPTER

42

In *April 1947, a Soviet* officer called Sugihara aside. He
told him in Russian that he would let Chiune go back
to Japan now. He didn't give a reason.

Chiune told Yukiko that they were finally going
back to Japan. A feeling of great joy spread through her
entire body.

They were taken to a very small cargo ship, where it
was necessary to climb a straight ladder up and down
from the deck. It took several days, but finally the ship
arrived in Vladivostok.

In Vladivostok they were loaded onto a Japanese
ship called *Koan Maru* that was used to repatriate people
to Japan. All around, people spoke Japanese.

The Sugiharas stood together at the railing and looked intensely for the first sight of Japan. Chiune hid his apprehension and Yukiko began to cry at the first sight of Hakata Port. The children were so surprised to see their mother cry that they watched her instead of focusing on the land that the ship was slowly approaching.

Mr. Sugihara was overwhelmed that he was seeing his homeland again and would see cherry blossoms once more. Somehow, he and Yukiko, Hiroki, Chiaki, Haruki, and Setsuko were all alive.

Then Yukiko whispered. "It's Japan. We've come back to Japan."

CHAPTER

43

Chiune and Yukiko were exhausted and had almost no savings when they returned to Japan. The first thing they did was to visit Yukiko's mother in Kanuki and put the children in school. Because Hiroki, Chiaki, and Haruki were often heard speaking to each other in Romanian or German, the children at the local elementary school thought that they were foreign children speaking in exotic languages.

Sugihara informed the Foreign Ministry of his return and apprehensively waited to be summoned for a meeting. He did his best to appear calm, but both he and his wife had long been expecting the past to catch up with them. They knew the time would soon come.

One day, Chiune received an official letter from the Foreign Ministry requesting his immediate appearance before the vice foreign minister.

Sugihara dressed carefully. He squeezed his wife's hands, then left.

While she waited for him to return, Yukiko realized that they both had held on to hope that the issuing of visas in Lithuania would be forgotten. Perhaps — as nothing had been said to them about it through the entire war — it really had been forgotten. Perhaps!

Later, Yukiko heard Chiune open the door. She went to meet him. He looked exhausted and sad. She waited for him to speak, dreading what he would tell her.

He sat down and quietly described how he was called into the office of Vice Foreign Minister Okazaki and told, "As we no longer have a post for you, please resign. We can no longer take you under our wing!"

Chiune and Yukiko looked into each other's eyes. A shadow had fallen across Sugihara's face. Seeing the dark shadow, Yukiko couldn't look at him any longer and turned away.

Chiune had no choice but to accept the decision of the Ministry. He resigned and was given a small retirement settlement. Yukiko had to learn to cook and keep house because they no longer had any servants to help.

Mr. Sugihara was now forty-seven. There were shortages everywhere in postwar Japan. Food was rationed. Jobs were hard to come by, also. At first, the only job he could find was as a door-to-door salesman, selling light bulbs. Then he worked as a translator and a sales representative.

After a while, Chiune told Yukiko the more complete version of that terrible meeting with Vice Foreign Minister Okazaki. That day, he had arrived at the office of the vice foreign minister and presented himself to the secretary who had told him to take a seat and that he would be called soon.

His back had been straight as he had sat quietly until he was called into the office. Then, Vice Foreign Minister Okazaki greeted him. Without mincing words, Okazaki told him it was because of his actions in Lithuania that they could no longer keep him aboard.

Of course. They had known long ago that this might happen. Afterward, Sugihara never showed emotion to anyone. He lived with special patience.

One day little Haruki came home from school and out of the blue told his mother that he thought heaven was a beautiful place. He told her he didn't want to become an adult and would die while he was still a child. He would go to heaven and become an angel.

Yukiko explained that if he went to heaven, she and his father would be very sad. Haruki looked up at her solemnly. He promised that he would come back again if she ever called him. With that, the strange conversation with the little boy ended.

Several days later, Haruki returned from school pale and suffering from a bad headache. Abruptly, his nose began to bleed. Mr. and Mrs. Sugihara and the two older boys stayed beside Haruki's bed. The doctor came to treat him, but couldn't help. Before morning, Haruki died.

Mr. Sugihara went out into his small garden and stood alone. He had lost his career, been disgraced and shamed, now his youngest son, the one born in Kaunas and weakened by the harsh internment camps after the war, his Bright Spirit — had died. He wondered if perhaps Haruki had been sent by God as a messenger to remind him to help the Jewish refugees in Kaunas. Perhaps after the help had been given, Haruki's mission had been accomplished, and God had wanted Haruki with him in heaven again.

Shiimbo shiite seiko suru — success comes through overcoming adversity. Yes, perhaps that explained everything.

Epilogue

One day in 1951, four years after Haruki's death, Yukiko told Sugihara that she was pregnant. She told him that she believed that this baby was the reincarnation of Haruki.

She gave birth to a boy. They named him Nobuki, which means Long Life.

Although his career had been destroyed and his child had died, Chiune Sugihara never regretted the action he had taken in Lithuania by issuing thousands of visas to desperate people. Despite grief and disgrace, he managed to find other work, however humbling, so that he could support his family. After briefly working as a salesman and translator, he worked for the American occupation forces in Japan, then for a textile company. Yukiko learned to live without servants or luxury.

In 1960, because of his knowledge of the Russian language, he took a job in Moscow for a trading company and then, also in Moscow, he worked for an export plant. He often took long walks in birch forests outside of Moscow, even though the temperature sometimes reached 30 degrees below zero. Chiune lived and worked in Moscow until he retired in 1976.

Except for the biannual visits to Japan, Chiune was separated from Yukiko and his children during most of these years. After the death of her son, and then the death of her sister, Setsuko, two years later, Yukiko was stricken with low blood pressure and lived with severe anxiety, grief, and loneliness.

Through the long, lonely years Sugihara often wondered whether or not the visas he had signed in Lithuania had saved any lives. But, he had no way of knowing. Then, in 1968, twenty-eight years after he had been in Lithuania, Sugihara received a telephone call asking him to visit the Israeli Embassy.

When he was shown into the Israeli ambassador's office, he encountered an aged man. The man held out a piece of paper, and asked if he remembered the paper.

Sugihara touched the dirty, worn, old document and recognized it as one of his visas. The man told him he was Yehoshua Nishri. He was one of the Jewish representatives who met with Mr. Sugihara in Kaunas to discuss his situation and that of the other Jews gathered at the consulate.

He grabbed Mr. Sugihara's hand. Tears welled in his eyes. He told Chiune that many Jewish survivors had received his visas. He explained that he'd tried to locate him since the end of the war but that, until now, the search had been in vain.

They realized that the survivors had been searching the records of the Japanese Foreign Ministry for Sempo Sugihara, not Chiune, and that was why no information had been found. Chiune had always felt that if he had even saved one refugee's life, it would have all been worth it. Now he learned that many, many lives had been saved.

A short time later, Chiune and Yukiko were invited to visit Israel. On arrival, they immediately smelled the sweet odor of orange blossoms. There, they met Zorach Warhaftig again. Warhaftig had been the head of the five-man committee of refugees who'd conferred with Sugihara. Warhaftig's eyes filled with tears. He took Sugihara's hands, calling him "our emissary of God."

Laughing, he told Sugihara that he had twenty-five grandchildren. Warhaftig had become the Israeli minister of religion and was one of the original signers of the Israeli Declaration of Independence.

In 1976, Chiune and Yukiko retired to a small house in Kamakura, Japan, close to Kamakura Mountain. In old age, as his health failed, Sugihara would often sit at his piano and play "A Maiden's Prayer." He and Yukiko walked in the mountains. Often they walked without speaking. *Ishin denshin* — you speak through the heart; words were unnecessary.

In 1985, after being recognized and honored, a monument to Sugihara was erected on a hillside in Jerusalem and he was awarded the Righteous Among the Nations medal by Yad Vashem, Israel's Holocaust Memorial and Museum. Unfortunately, Sugihara was too ill to attend the dedication during which the Japanese flag, the Rising Sun, flew next to the Israeli flag, the Star of David.

Also in 1985, a Japanese civic group formally apologized to Chiune, Yukiko, and their children, and Chiune was awarded the Nagasaki Peace Prize.

In 1989, a Jewish journalist from the *Forward* newspaper went to interview Yukiko Sugihara, who was being honored by the Anti-Defamation League of B'nai

B'rith — an organization in New York that fights anti-Semitism and all forms of bigotry. The journalist suddenly broke down during the interview. She just sat and sobbed. Yukiko and her son Hiroki, who was acting as translator, sat respectfully and waited. The journalist's name was Masha Leon. Her maiden name was Masha Bernstein.

Masha explained that until that moment, she believed she and her mother had been helped by entities, by anonymous consulates, by organizations like the Jewish Joint Distribution Committee, HIAS/Hebrew Immigration Aid Society, the International Red Cross, the Jewish Labor Committee, and the Japanese Consulate in Kaunas. Now, almost fifty years later, Masha realized that their lives had been saved by individuals. Masha and her mother had received visa No. 1882, and now she was looking into the eyes of Mrs. Sugihara, the wife of the man whose signature had made it possible for them to escape from Europe.

Of Poland's 3.3 million prewar Jews, over three million had been killed by the Nazis. Masha and Zelda and Matvey Bernstein were among the very few Polish Jews who had survived, and Masha and Zelda had escaped from Europe, thanks to their Sugihara visa.

As Masha herself explains, "And here I was sitting

across from a woman who, had she said to her husband, 'Don't do it, you're putting your life in danger. You're putting your career in danger. You're putting your children in danger. You're sabotaging your future,' he wouldn't have issued the visas. So, in effect, I owe my life to Yukiko just as much as I owe it to Mr. Sugihara."

Solly Ganor went to Israel after the war. In liberated Lithuania, fewer than 4,000 to 6,000 Jews remained alive from a total Jewish prewar population of 235,000. More than ninety-six percent had perished. Solly, his father, and his sister were three of the survivors.

Every year, during April, the entire world celebrates Yom Hashoa, the Day of Holocaust Remembrance. Solly described in his memoir *Light One Candle* what it's like to have survived the Holocaust: ". . . Something inside of me died. Although my body survived intact, my spirit was crippled. In my mind's eye I saw myself as the trunk of a tree that had survived a forest fire. Black and charred beyond recognition with all my branches gone. I managed to sprout new branches in order to live, but the old ones never grew back."

After the war, Solly discovered that on December 25, 1944 (his father's birthday) his mother had died of typhoid fever in Stutthof. He realized that his father's supernatural vision of his wife's death had been true. Solly's sister Fanny survived and told him that she had been applying compresses to their mother's brow when she died.

On the hillside overlooking Yad Vashem, a tree was planted in honor of Chiune Sugihara. Seventy Sugihara visa recipients attended. One bragged that he had even more grandchildren than Zorach Warhaftig; he had thirty.

In addition, an entire forest of trees was planted in Sugihara's name south of Jerusalem.

It is estimated that Consul Sugihara issued 6,000 Japanese transit visas. An estimated 40,000 descendants of his visa recipients, now known as "Sugihara Survivors," are alive because of his extraordinary courage. This was one of the largest rescues of Jews in the Holocaust.

On July 30, 1986, Chiune died. In her memoir *Visas For Life*, Yukiko remembers: ". . . He left for Heaven. His life had passed away, and I noticed the shimmer of the mid-summer sea, which Chiune loved, reflecting through the window. He once had said to me: 'I didn't do anything special. . . . I made my own decisions, that's all. I followed my own conscience and listened to it.'"

His ashes were buried in Kamakura Cemetery.

He is honored in Japan by a large memorial and park in his hometown of Yaotsu. The monument stands in a pond. The pond symbolizes humanity, the rings around the pond symbolize the widening ripple effect of an act of kindness.

AUTHOR'S
ACKNOWLEDGMENTS

The author is very grateful to the following: The Sugihara family, especially Yukiko Sugihara and her fine book *Visas for Life*; Solly Ganor and his powerful book *Light One Candle*; Hillel Levine's *In Search of Sugihara*; Masha Leon, Eric Saul, Amy Fiske, the Simon Wiesenthal Center, Los Angeles; the U.S. Holocaust Memorial Museum, Washington, D.C.; Hawthornden International Writers Retreat, Laswade, Scotland; William and Shirley Greenwald, Dorothy Greenwald, and Thor Gold.